Crack Cocaine, Crime, and Women

Drugs, Health, and Social Policy Series

Edited by James A. Inciardi
University of Delaware

About This Series . . .

The Sage **Drugs, Health, and Social Policy Series** provides students and professionals in the fields of substance abuse, AIDS, public health, and criminal justice access to current research, programs, and policy issues particular to their specialties. Each year, four new volumes will focus on a topic of national significance.

Crack Cocaine, Crime, and Women

Legal, Social, and Treatment Issues

Sue Mahan

Drugs, Health, and Social Policy Series
Volume 4

SAGE Publications
International Educational and Professional Publisher
Thousand Oaks London New Delhi

For information address:

SAGE Publications, Inc.
2455 Teller Road
Thousand Oaks, California 91320
E-mail: order@sagepub.com

SAGE Publications Ltd.
6 Bonhill Street
London EC2A 4PU
United Kingdom

SAGE Publications India Pvt. Ltd.
M-32 Market
Greater Kailash I
New Delhi 110 048 India

Printed in the United States of America

Library of Congress Cataloging-in-Publication Data

Mahan, Sue.
    Crack cocaine, crime, and women : legal, social, and treatment issues / Sue Mahan.
        p.   cm. — (Drugs, health, and social policy ; 4)
    Includes bibliographical references (p. 79) and index.
    ISBN 0-7619-0141-8 (cloth : alk. paper). — ISBN 0-7619-0142-6 (pbk. : alk. paper)
    1. Women—Drug use—United States. 2. Cocaine habit—United States. 3. Crack (Drug)—United States. 4. Drug abuse and crime--United States. 5. Drug abuse in pregnancy—United States. I. Title. II. Series.
HV5824.W6M34   1996
362.29'18'082—dc20   96-25309

    This book is printed on acid-free paper.

96 97 98 99 00 10 9 8 7 6 5 4 3 2 1

Sage Production Editor: Michèle Lingre

Table of Contents

Acknowledgments

We appreciate the support of Volusia County Judge Hubert L. Grimes. The cooperation of Anti-Recidivist Effort (ARE) Directors Nellie Allen, Leon Gillis, and Barry Simms also is greatly appreciated.

In addition, we would like to offer appreciation to numerous "crack mothers" who participated in our study, not only those whose interviews are recorded in Part I but also many others. Without their assistance, this book would not have come to life.

Prologue

Work began on this book at the University of Central Florida—Daytona Beach in 1989. It has been a collaborative effort with many contributors, beginning with the initiative of Della Alice Prestwood. She gathered preliminary data in a community survey to establish the extent and nature of the local problem of crack mothers. The next study, in 1990, considered the issue of treatment and provided a case study of a program that had been developed for pregnant women addicted to cocaine. Also in 1990, Julie Howkins examined the legal issues concerning pregnancy and criminalization. Her work included a survey of state legislators. Throughout 1993, the author interviewed crack-addicted women about their lifestyles. In 1995, Valencia Gallon provided legal research to expand the analysis of the criminalization of pregnancy. Also in 1995 and in 1996, Andrea Holmes collected and organized the extensive bibliography for this book. From 1989 through 1996, when the book was completed, Jackie Connelly kept the project going with assistance and editing.

Our efforts are offered in the memory of Alice Prestwood, who planted the seed but did not live to see the fruit.

Introduction

This is a book about women addicted to crack cocaine. It describes lives in a subculture called Crackworld. It explains the legal issues that have developed because of women's involvement in addiction-related crime, including a gender-specific crime called fetal endangerment. It also explores treatment programs for addicted women who have children. A common street name for crack cocaine is "rock." "Rock stars" see the glamorous side of the crack market, with its money, power, and pleasure. "Rock stars," however, become "rock monsters" trapped in a lifestyle of degradation, criminality, and uncontrollable impulses.

Since 1989, when crack mothers first attracted public attention, until the present, the issue of "crack moms" has been examined from many perspectives. There is still no end to the controversy about the problem. It is the purpose of this book to bring together divergent views rather than contribute to the controversy. The approach is threefold: subcultural, legal, and treatment. The book is divided into three parts, with each part further subdivided into three sections. The first section covers the background concepts and issues that are important to review with regard to each of the three approaches. The second section includes a systematic analysis of the way these issues affect persons, policies, and programs. The third section contains a case study that explores the concepts within a real-life situation.

The lifestyles of crack abusers in decaying neighborhoods is described in Part I as a subculture called Crackworld. The lifestyle can be found in large urban areas but also in smaller cities and elsewhere. The concepts and issues are socioeconomic. The combination of violence and degradation that is found in Crackworld is especially costly for women.

The applications of legal options of dealing with crack abusers are considered in Part II as they relate to the criminalization of pregnancy. The criminal alternatives in effect include charges of child abuse or neglect, manslaughter, or delivery of a controlled substance to a minor. Involuntary detention may be invoked as a criminal or a civil option. In some states, laws have been rewritten to apply particularly to fetal endangerment. Considering a fetus as a person goes beyond Supreme Court decisions and has not been upheld in appeals courts.

The development of treatment programs is the subject of Part III. Treatment for crack users must address two special patterns. First, the crack lifestyle includes compulsive dysfunctional sexuality that may be little understood and difficult to treat. Second, crack users are more likely than other substance abusers to have been victims of extreme violence. Despite these distinctions, much of what has been successful in treatment for other addictions has been applied to crack-abusing patients with overall positive outcomes. Unfortunately, even though the models are available and might be applied successfully in theory, in practice there are few or no programs available for those long-term, drug-abusing mothers who are most in need of them.

Explanations offered in this book about women who smoke crack come from a broad range of interests. The descriptions were developed over a long span of study. The overview is intended to be both informative and useful. The three different perspectives on the prob-lem—subcultural, legal, and treatment—demonstrate the complexity of the issues. Social workers, criminal justice authorities, and treatment providers, all of whom must deal with cocaine-abusing mothers, have more in common than often appears.

More important, everyone in the United States has more in common with the problems faced by addicted mothers than we may possibly imagine. Our position in the future will depend on how we treat the infants and children of today. To most politicians and voters, treatment policies are not considered to be as important as legal policies, yet without concern for how treatment is provided, we pay a high cost in crime and wasted resources. Often, programs meant to be preventive are considered expendable and likely to be the first cut when budgets are trimmed. Most significant of all, the obvious plight of those living in decaying, run-down neighborhoods is thought to be nobody's problem but their own.

The children of Crackworld are everybody's children, and their mothers are a humanistic concern. There are no easy answers to providing for their needs, but some things have become obvious. The problem of babies born to substance-abusing mothers cannot be solved by pitting the interests of mothers against those of infants. Policy and resources must provide for their common interests and mutual well-being.

1. Crackworld

As the use of crack spread across the United States, women became involved in drug use as never before. Various academic and government studies showed higher rates of dependence for women than for men (Inciardi, Lockwood, & Pottieger, 1993; National Institute of Justice, 1990). During the 1980s, a picture of the lifestyle of crack addicts emerged from these and other studies. The image of a subculture surfaced, a microcosm that was part of the larger culture but within it. The customs, beliefs, and traditions of another world became common within that subculture. A large proportion of members are female, and sexual exchanges have a central role in the day-to-day lives of those in this subculture, which in this book is called Crackworld.

The Subculture:
Concepts and Issues

The Crack Plague

The first mention of "crack" appeared in 1985 on a back page, in a largely unnoticed article of *The New York Times*. In the next 11 months, crack took on a life of its own. More than 1,000 stories in which crack figured prominently appeared in the major United States media. In 1986, both CBS and NBC produced prime time reports about crack. In these and other stories, the implication was clear: Crack led the user almost immediately into a nightmare world from which there was little likelihood of escape (Inciardi, 1992).

The nickname "crack" comes from the crackling sound the drug makes when it is smoked. In the most common method for making crack, cocaine hydrochloride powder is converted into crack by cooking it in a mixture of baking soda and water, then heat-drying. The hard substance that remains is broken into "rocks" and smoked (Abadinsky, 1989).

Crack is known by many names, such as "hard white" and "flavor." There are "bricks," "boulders," and "eight-balls" (large rocks or slabs of crack), "doo-wap" (two rocks), and "crumbs," "shake," and "kibbles & bits" (for smaller pieces). There is the "dope man" or "bond man" who can deliver a "cookie" (large quantity), which he carries in his "bomb bag" to the "crack house." The dope man may also deal or "juggle" his crack on the street (Inciardi, 1992).

In many crack houses, the drug may be displayed on boards, tables, or mirrors, whereas in the street, crack is packaged in small glass vials or plastic bags. In a few locales, these bags are sealed or stamped with a brand name, affording the illusion of quality control and giving the buyer a specific name for which to ask. In New York City, crack labels such as "White Cloud," "Conan," and "Hardball" were reported. In Miami, researchers found labels including "Cigarette" (from a type of speedboat), "Biscayne Babe" (for Biscayne Boulevard prostitutes), "Bogey" (of the movie *Key Largo*), and "Noriega's Holiday" (for the former Panamanian dictator) (Inciardi, 1992).

Crack has been called the fast food variety of cocaine. It is cheap and easy to conceal, and it vaporizes with practically no odor. The gratification it brings is swift, an intense, almost sexual euphoria that lasts less than five minutes. Smoking cocaine, as opposed to snorting it, results in more immediate and direct absorption of the drug. It produces a quicker and more compelling high, sometimes called a "rush."

By this method of ingestion, the drug vaporizes from the heat and is inhaled. The nature by which the drug is taken into the bloodstream is believed to increase both the abuse liability and dependence potential. There is a risk of acute toxic reactions to crack, including brain seizure, cardiac irregularities, respiratory paralysis, paranoid psychosis, and pulmonary dysfunction (Inciardi, 1992, p. 127).

Subculture

Although using crack never became popular in the general population, its appeal in the majority of the nation's inner cities has endured. There is little reason to expect change for the better (Inciardi, 1992, chap. 4), for in the decaying communities of the United States, a picture has emerged of a culture of powerlessness (Boyle & Anglin, 1993).

This culture is the epitome of poverty, ethnic segregation, and polarized gender relations. It is not an aberration of life in the United States but a reflection of it (Ouellet, Wiebel, Jimenez, & Johnson, 1993). The subculture of Crackworld shows the underside of the American dream. Our society sustains classist, racist, and sexist public policies that reflect the interests of those in power. For those facing the results of these policies, the lifestyle is dominated by unmet economic, social, and personal needs.

Crackworld is found in a community with problems, poverty, crime, child neglect, homelessness, and drug addiction being only the most obvious. These neighborhoods suffer from poor community health. The churches, the press, and the family have lost power. People here exist on the economic margins, more and more dependent on the will and decisions of outside forces.

Although there are crack users in glamour professions and the upper and middle classes, these users are not considered members of the Crackworld subculture. By the nature of their more affluent lifestyles, crack users with means made the cocaine industry prosper. Poor drug users and sellers have been the most visible, most often arrested, and most often filmed and written about (Williams, 1992).

Along with the media, academic and government researchers are also likely to study the lifestyles of crack users who are the poorest members of their communities. Many are homeless or have only temporary living arrangements. Few have marketable job skills or significant work experience (Koester & Schwartz, 1993). There are others who are less disabled by crack but whose lives are affected by using the drug. Those who use the drug less frequently and those whose resources keep them off the street are not likely to be included in stories about crack, either in the media or in academic research, but their contribution to the subculture must be considered.

Although crack dealers commonly have regular, neighborhood customers, they cannot depend on them for the large sums of money involved in the crack trade. The crack market depends on drive-up customers who live outside Crackworld and go there to get drugs. The market also depends on proceeds from selling stolen goods, which crack addicts use to pay for the drug. The market for stolen goods is fed by those with means who want to buy luxury goods at low prices. These key players are not always visible in the subculture, but they are there.

Others who are key players in Crackworld are law enforcement agents and city and county authorities. Although it may appear that those in authority are merely passing through Crackworld because they do not reside there, their impact is immeasurable.

Both for those who use crack and for those who profit from it, one of the important characteristics of the crack subculture found by researchers is a lack of peer pressure to moderate drug use. The economics of crack houses encourage immoderate use. Dealers and those in charge of crack houses exploit desperate users. Interpersonal relations are often dominated by intimidation and fear (Zinberg, 1984). Crackworld portrays the classical cyclical pattern of crime financing use, use encouraging more use, and more use encouraging more crime (Inciardi et al., 1993, p. 131).

Outside cultural messages promote neediness and dissatisfaction among the members of Crackworld. Their lifestyles, being marginal to the rest of the economy, lead to a reality very different from the one they see on television or hear about in the news. Not only are their lives bleak, but they also are reminded at every turn that others do not suffer from the same fate. Their dissatisfaction may fester when all avenues to that envisioned reality are blocked and no opportunities for real economic change present themselves.

At the same time, street markets flourish as a result of massive importation of cocaine. Despite the most stringent measures to rid American society of the scourge of drug addiction, the quantity and quality of drugs available in street markets has increased. As law enforcement has developed more systematic methods to break up the crack market, drug traffickers have developed more sophisticated and effective methods of transporting and distributing their product. Some neighborhoods, through their own organized efforts, have managed to rid themselves of the crack market. Although that may save one community from annihilation, the market only moves on; it is not destroyed. Often the market thrives by moving from one location to another whenever there are efforts at control. The same is true at the international level: When a supplier is wiped out in one location, another source opens up in another location and takes over the newly vacated position in the market.

The broader culture also maintains a well-paying marketplace for sexual services, making prostitution a likely source of money to buy crack. The drug market flourishes from the money that nonusers of crack pay to prostitutes who are addicted. Sometimes a prostitute may support, with her earnings, her own habit and those of others with whom she is involved.

Residents of Crackworld also have lost alternatives in the legal employment market because of structural changes in the economy. Throughout the 1980s, low-income, unskilled workers were displaced by changes in the economy and technological innovations. Large corporate enterprises that controlled the economy had no interest in poorly educated, ill-prepared workers in low-income communities. Intense competition for jobs was fueled by an influx of immigration from the Caribbean, Latin America, and Asia.

Added to the community disorganization is the degradation of municipal services supporting health, housing, and education for the poor. Many community organizations now found in inner-city areas were initiated in the early 1970s. After more than 20 years, many of them have broken down under the strain of poverty and pathology. Departments of welfare are notoriously understaffed and overextended. Citizens who never visit and know nothing about Crackworld are unconcerned that so many social ills have been concentrated in isolated neighborhoods. Crack subcultures therefore continue to be found amid the ruins of American society (Zinberg, 1984).

Inner Cities

According to the Bureau of Justice Statistics 1990 National Household Survey on Drug Abuse, the prevalence of illegal drug use is higher in large than in small metropolitan areas and nonmetropolitan areas. Of respondents in large metropolitan areas, 15% admitted to illicit drug use in the past year, compared with 13% of respondents in small metropolitan areas and 11% of nonmetropolitan respondents. Marijuana and cocaine are more likely to be used in metropolitan areas. In rural areas, the most widely abused drug is alcohol. The prevalence of use of other drugs such as inhalants may be higher in rural areas than elsewhere (Bureau of Justice Statistics, 1992). Illicit drug users outside the large metropolitan areas in the United States are largely unstudied and ignored.

Rapid increase in crack use after the mid-1980s has been described as a symptom of the ongoing social disintegration of America's inner cities (Koester & Schwartz, 1993). Some researchers assumed that the advent of crack cocaine was related to the collapse of formal and informal social controls in urban areas (Maher & Curtis, 1995). Most of what is known about Crackworld comes from research done in deteriorating areas of large metropolitan centers.

When the media or researchers studied the users of and use of crack, they focused on the underside of society and centered on urban decay. Much of what is known has to do with poverty and socioeconomic factors of the lower classes, because crack users with means usually have not been included in the studies. The users in what is being called Crackworld may not always depend on crack as a means of finding oblivion. In the near future, a different drug may likely become popular. At such a time, the subculture may change because of the pharmacological effects of a different addiction, but without change in the socioeconomic factors, there is little reason to expect the change to be for the better.

We are likely to see increasing violence in the future crackworlds. The violence accompanying cocaine and heroin use has continued to increase since the 1980s. Despite increased arrests of drug sellers, community safety in inner cities has declined substantially in recent years. The effects of law enforcement efforts to stop drug markets in the inner city have, in fact, significantly contributed to a decline in the economic well-being of most users and sellers. Other unintended consequences include the perpetuation of an environment of poor health and increased risk of death at an early age, as well as a weakening of family relationships.

Results are similar nationwide. Jails and prisons bulge with inner-city crack users and dealers arrested and convicted on a variety of charges, but especially for sales. Few officials believe that inner-city neighborhoods are much safer because so many crack users and dealers have been incarcerated. General agreement exists that community safety in the inner city and other neighborhoods declined substantially during the latter half of the 1980s.

After more than a decade of crack marketing, inner-city drug users are likely to continue their addiction cycles, whether or not the object of addiction is crack. They also can be expected to continue depleting their economic well-being without positive expectations for the future. Inner-city addicts have few opportunities for rehabilitation to legitimate activities, and they continue to overwhelm the criminal justice, correctional, drug treatment, and health care systems.

Inner-city communities have the worst measures on virtually all indices of public health. Cocaine and heroin abusers are considered at high risk for almost all health measures. They contribute a disproportionate share of all persons who are "ill," regardless of the specific sickness. Crack users typically neglect regular nutrition, sleep, and preventive health practices. The drug acts as an appetite suppressant, so users frequently spend food money for drugs and eat "sweets" (sodas and candy) rather than a variety of foods. Normal sleep and rest are not routine. During runs of cocaine or crack use, users may be awake for several days. Users typically seek medical attention only for acute and life-threatening episodes.

Family formation, child rearing, and responsible parenting are very difficult, if not impossible, during daily use of hard drugs. Children of substance abusers are at high risk for similar outcomes as they grow up.

It is apparent that the already adverse conditions existing in the inner city have been further aggravated by the growth and violence of the crack market. The crack economy has become a major factor in expanding the criminal underclass in the inner city, enriching a few upper-level distributors but impoverishing thousands of compulsive users. The drug economy is likely to continue to expand, with more street sellers and low-level distributors. Because of the flexible organizational structure of crack distribution groups in the inner city, there is every indication that violence associated with the drug market will increase (Johnson, Williams, Dei, & Sanabria, 1990).

Opium Dens, Speakeasies, and Shooting Galleries

It is not surprising that researchers found another subculture among crack cocaine users. Historically, users of illegal or illicit substances have congregated to buy and use drugs and to enjoy getting high together. A lifestyle with different customs and shared experiences is likely to develop among them. If the substance is illegal or is shunned by other members of society, the values that hold users together may be in opposition to the larger culture that rejects them.

As in Crackworld, the subculture of opium addicts was centered on a local place where users gathered for smoking. The opium den, "dive," or "joint" was not only a place for smoking but also a meeting place, a sanctuary. For members of the underworld, it was a place to gather in relative safety, to enjoy a smoke of opium, hashish, or tobacco with friends and associates. Opium dens varied in quality from very comfortable to very primitive. To some users, they were no more than places to go to forget.

During Prohibition, speakeasies could be found almost everywhere. They were of many types, from urban "clip joints" to brownstone residences operated under the guise of "clubs." In rural areas, there were "roadhouses." Some were elegant and others were shacks; most were somewhere in between. Speakeasies left an image of drunkenness, sexual impropriety, and gambling.

For the better part of the 20th century, addicts who inject drugs have gotten high in neighborhood "shooting galleries." According to Inciardi, "galleries" are considered the least desirable and most dangerous places to use heroin, amphetamines, cocaine, and other injectable psychoactive drugs. Nevertheless, for intravenous (IV) drug users, use of "shooting galleries" is routine and commonplace (Inciardi et al., 1993).

Crack Houses

Crack sellers hang out on busy corners to be available to drive-up customers, but these users have means and do not take on the lifestyle of the subculture. They use crack "anywhere" and "everywhere." Crack addicts who cannot smoke in their own homes, cars, or rented rooms are left to use the drug on the street. Sometimes they use the services of a "house." As the popularity of crack grew, in some neighborhoods users began to congregate in designated houses and abandoned buildings.

A convergence of shooting galleries and crack houses is of grave concern because of the high degree of sexual activity that takes place in crack houses (Ouellet et al., 1993). In many instances, crack smokers and IV drug users are drawn to the same locations for the many kinds of illegal and illicit services that are sold there. Both the sharing of common equipment for injection of IV drugs and the likelihood of unprotected sex associated with the use of crack are activities strongly linked with high rates of infectious diseases, especially hepatitis and AIDS.

Crack houses are organized places where cocaine smokers can find the privacy and paraphernalia needed to smoke and sometimes cook cocaine into crack or rocks. Crack houses may also be places to buy drugs. Compared to shooting galleries, crack houses are more likely to be the scene of sex, stealing, bizarre behavior, begging, and/or violence. The willingness to do just about anything for a drug is more often attributed to users of crack houses than to users of shooting galleries.

Crack houses are used by smokers who need to hide this activity from those with whom they live and by those who have no place else to go (Ouellet et al., 1993). Inciardi estimates that there were no fewer than 700 operating crack houses in the greater Miami area in the early 1990s. He quotes a Miami crack dealer, or "kingrat," who describes crack houses as "a carnival of vice . . . home to the wretched, the depraved, and the perverted . . [who] will do anything for a hit on the stem" (1993, p. 39).

The term "crack house" can mean a number of different things. The same types of places can be known, among other names, as "smoke houses" or "base houses," depending on the site. They can be places to use, sell, or both. They also can be places to manufacture and package crack. The location may be a house, an apartment, a small shack at the back of an empty lot, an abandoned building, or even the rusting hulk of a discarded automobile (Inciardi et al., 1993).

The most common kind of crack houses are personal residences where small groups of people gather regularly to smoke crack. The operators of these places may not call them "crack houses" because payment is made only with crack. The visitors to other types of crack houses are "customers" who pay in regular currency (Inciardi et al., 1993).

Inciardi developed a typology of the crack houses he found in Miami in 1992. The following are seven general types of crack houses, with the names they were given in the Miami Crackworld.

1. Castles are fortified structures where large quantities of crack are manufactured, packaged, and sold. Users are not permitted inside.

2. Base houses are all-purpose drug joints. A variety of drugs are available. Sex is not part of the activities.

3. Resorts are small apartments adapted for crack use. The kitchen is used for cooking rock, at least one bedroom is set aside for sex, and the living space is used for selling and smoking.

4. Brothels are places where crack and sex are both sold by a dealer/pimp. The prostitute is the house girl (or boy), who receives payment in the form of crack and room and board.

5. Residence houses are the most common form of crack house. They are used for friends to gather and smoke. Crack is not sold. Visitors share crack with the resident of the property in return for having a place to smoke or turn a trick.

6. Graveyards are rooms in abandoned buildings and shacks. No one actually owns the place; use is based on squatters' rights.

7. Organized houses are few in number and far more controlled than other types. They are carefully managed places of business where strict order is maintained (Inciardi, 1992, chap. 4).

According to Williams (1992), crack houses are open "24-7," 24 hours a day, 7 days a week, to a steady stream of people—some high, some not; some men, some women. More than 40% of crack house regulars are young women, most of them Latina and African American, some in their teens.

Among the most extreme and offbeat aspects of crack house life are the sexual activities and ventures that transpire there. Selling sexual services is central. The risks for the transactions include physical abuse, violence, sexually transmitted diseases, and arrest. Long-term concerns for those involved include health care, child care, and lack of legitimate income (Inciardi et al., 1993).

Sex for Crack Exchanges

In crack houses, payment occurs before, during, and after sexual services. In the crack house, both the customer and the prostitute use drugs, and the exchange may last for 30 minutes or more. Men in crack houses receive and control sexual attention (Inciardi et al., 1993, p. 76).

Prostitutes in Crackworld seldom depend on pimps: Crack is the pimp (Inciardi et al., 1993, p. 85). Women trading sex in a crack house must give a share, sometimes all, of the drugs, money, or sex to the owner of the house. The women are paying to use the house and, indirectly, for protection. As long as they remain in the house, crack whores are secure in a source of drugs, protection from the weather and other elements, and having other crack users with whom to associate. That protection costs the prostitute her dignity and self-respect. In exchange for drugs, a crack whore faces rape and physical abuse at the hands of other crack users and the operator of the house.

The tendency of crack users to engage in high-frequency sex with numerous anonymous partners is a feature of crack dependence and crack house life in myriad locales. Crack is purported to engender some sort of "hypersexuality" (Inciardi et al., 1993). Crack seems to have a disinhibiting and degrading effect on women and men alike (p. 71). Dysfunctional sexuality is the result of the pharmacological elements of crack cocaine and the sociocultural elements of Crackworld (Inciardi et al., 1993, p. 96).

It appears that men are more likely than women to find that cocaine enhances their sexual desire. Social conditions may convene to produce this impression. Many prostitutes find that, rather than acting as an aphrodisiac, crack reduces their interest in sex (Feldman, Espada, Penn, & Byrd, 1993). This is likely to be a result of social conditions for women. Many prostitutes report that men high on crack are unable to function sexually. Some researchers believe that this sexual frustration often leads to voyeuristic behavior and violent humiliation of vulnerable females (Bourgois & Dunlap, 1993). Individuals most dependent on crack are those most likely to be involved in degrading sexual encounters and also those least able to insist on safer sex practices (Ratner, 1993).

Women who use drugs and who use sex to obtain them have a higher rate of contracting HIV/AIDS infection than men who engage in risky behavior (CDC, Freeman, Rodriguez, & French , 1994). Studies show that rates of HIV infection among prison entrants are higher for women than for men. There is a serious lack of services to deal with women's special health care needs in most prison systems (Osborn, 1990). As Inciardi and others have stressed, the unique environment of crack houses has affected every aspect of the prostitution business.

Violence

The everyday context of life in Crackworld provides a high propensity for violence. Levels of violence have changed in recent years, affecting those in decaying neighborhoods most negatively. These changes are in response to shifting social and economic conditions as they manifest themselves at the local level (Maher & Curtis, 1995). Increases in crack-related violence in inner-city areas can be attributed to the breakdown of formal social controls such as law enforcement and informal social controls such as neighborhood vigilance. As businesses and successful members flee neighborhoods, the depletion of capital and human resources makes it impossible to sustain a formal economy. Participation in the drug business increases in a community when the residents think they have nothing to lose.

According to reports of the Bureau of Justice Statistics (1992), violence is used in drug markets to gain competitive advantage. It is desperate violence that governs all of street life in crack neighborhoods and drives the crack experience, rather than vice versa. Terror plays a wide role in the logic of street survival. Violence is part of an accepted and effective mode of functioning for those who participate in street life. Public displays of violence are channeled into gender-specific domains. Bullet wounds are defined as masculine, whereas razor-slash scars on the cheek are feminine. Violence is part of growing up; it is a rite of passage on the street (Bourgois & Dunlap, 1993).

Women who use crack and engage in prostitution are at high risk of being the victims of violent sex crimes. Men who use higher volumes of crack are more likely to be the perpetrators of violence (Goldstein, Belluci, Spunt, & Miller, 1991). In the crack market, buyers and dealers are at risk of assault, robbery, and death. Fear of getting cheated is a major concern, and arguments escalate quite easily to violence. Local and even regional markets are unstable and subject to aggressive bids for power (Inciardi et al., 1993).

Acts of drug-related violence can occur for a variety of reasons: territorial disputes among rival drug dealers; assaults and homicides committed within dealing and trafficking hierarchies as means of enforcing normative codes; robberies of drug dealers, often followed by extremely violent retaliations; elimination of informers; punishment for selling phony drugs; retribution for failing to pay one's debts; and general disputes over drugs or drug paraphernalia. Violence associated with disputes over drugs has been common to the drug scene since its inception (Inciardi, 1992, chap. 5).

Maher and Curtis (1995) found that all the female crack addicts they interviewed had been robbed and/or sexually assaulted or raped in the recent past. These prostitutes reported an increase in violent incidents committed by strangers and increased conflict in long-standing relationships. They acknowledged that in Crackworld, an atmosphere of intense competition for sexual markets and drastically deflated prices for sexual services led to considerable violence.

Cycle of Victimization

Many addicts in Crackworld were first exposed as children to their own parents' drug use in the home (Feldman et al., 1993). Few crack prostitutes experienced stable family lives. Almost without exception, they come from families of neglect and abuse. Sadly, their children's lives seem in many cases to be a repetition of their own family experiences (Bourgois & Dunlap, 1993). The Bureau of Justice Statistics succinctly reports, "Families with inconsistent discipline, drug-using parents, or distant relationships between parents and children may foster drug use" (1992, p. 22).

Among female addicts in Crackworld, traumatic experiences in early childhood were the norm rather than the exception. Most prostitutes have experienced psychological and physical abuse at the most vulnerable moments in their lives and often at very tender ages. Abused and neglected women may be more prone to suffer depression and perhaps to undergo psychiatric hospitalization as a consequence of those early childhood experiences. Not uncommonly, female drug users have been institutionalized in mental wards or juvenile delinquent facilities following their childhood rape traumas (Bourgois & Dunlap, 1993). Reaction to instances of sexual abuse usually includes bitterness and resentment.

"Violence begets violence" is one way to describe the cycle of violence that goes hand in hand with the cycle of victimization. Abused and neglected children have significantly greater risk of becoming delinquents and violent criminals. The intergenerational linkage between childhood victimization and later antisocial or criminal behavior, however, is far from certain: The intergenerational transmission of violence is not inevitable. Prevention programs and intervention strategies aimed at buffering at-risk children play a potentially important role in the reduction of future violent and self-destructive criminal behavior (Spatz-Widom, 1989).

There are mediating variables that act to buffer or protect abused or neglected children from developmental deficits and later delinquent and adult criminal behavior. Some of these protective factors are dispositional attributes. For example, calmness or self-esteem may work to place a child in a more favorable light and help her avoid abuse. Other protective factors come from environmental conditions. For example, if a child lives in close proximity to various members of her extended family or some other support network, they may help her to avoid abuse in her nuclear family. Biological dispositions also may serve as buffering factors. For example, if a child is sturdy and has a lot of stamina, she may avoid some abuse. Finally, there are positive events that help some children avoid later criminality. For example, winning a scholarship or a prize may provide a special opportunity for an abused child. Protective factors such as these act to mitigate the effects of early negative experiences (Spatz-Widom, 1989).

Even though not all child abuse can be prevented, there are clear policy goals contained within these buffering factors for helping victims. Mediating factors can be increased, strengthened, and supported.

Degradation

Prostitution long has been a controversial issue. Sometimes bitter social conflicts have arisen from the profound cultural contradiction on which prostitution is based. Men desire to ensure promiscuity for themselves and chastity for women. Men want to have sex with different women, and they want women who have sex with only one man. The male position provides an occupation for those females who are willing to go against culturally enforced chastity and sell sexual services to men who desire promiscuity. The contradiction is enforced by the degradation and humiliation to which prostitutes are commonly exposed.

The social order historically linked female worth and economic survival to marriage, and marriageability to chastity. Being outside marriage and family in the social order has put prostitutes at a disadvantage throughout much of history (Jolin, 1994). Prostitutes may get wealthy, but they are seldom, if ever, accepted within the support networks of the community.

As outsiders, they are at risk of isolation, powerlessness, and alienation. Being outside the family, a prostitute is vulnerable. Working outside the law, a prostitute cannot turn to law enforcement for protection. Living outside culturally accepted norms, a prostitute cannot look to community groups for support for her needs, such as housing; nor can she find protection from the risks of her trade related to health and abuse.

Inciardi and his colleagues (1993, p. 68) note that there are very real differences between prostitutes who use crack and crack users who exchange sex for drugs. The lowest status of all belongs to females who trade sex for drugs. To feed their compulsive need for crack, they remain in a position that carries with it humiliation and mean-spirited ridicule as characteristic of the trade (French, 1993).

The position of inferiority of crack whores as suppliers of sexual services is a result of the pattern of exchange. Payment to a prostitute in cash for her services infers that she has earned payment and has a right to it. When a man gives her cocaine, there are fewer rights on the part of the recipient. Women who exchange sex for crack are reduced to bartering from a very poor position. Old-time prostitutes complain, "These girls now have no self-respect" (Ouellet et al., 1993).

The highest status in Crackworld goes to those who deal, but do not use, illicit drugs such as cocaine or heroin. Women, who regularly trade sex directly for crack and act as key figures in the operation of crack houses, have the lowest status in Crackworld. They explain their behavior as out of their control, because they are driven to it from an obsessive desire for the drug (French, 1993).

There is no respect in Crackworld for crack whores. Street culture is profoundly sexist. It is commonly accepted in the subculture that vulnerable women deserve to be victimized. The females who barter sexual services, which are central to the crack house environment, are addicted and likely to be young, with little legitimate employment experience and no control over what happens to them. The violence these prostitutes experience simply reflects their neighborhood's reality (Bourgois & Dunlap, 1993).

Boyle and Anglin (1993) found that crack-addicted prostitutes could be divided into two categories, based on whether or not they sold sex before they began using crack. Those who were accustomed to working as professional prostitutes were less likely to be willing to exchange sex directly for crack. Those with little or no initiation into professional prostitution were less likely to use condoms, less likely to care for their appearance and health, and more likely to sleep in the streets or in homeless shelters.

Analysis of Interviews

Ethnographic Study of Crackworld

Those who have studied the subculture of crack use often have used the research methods of anthropologists. These tools include naturalistic observations and lengthy qualitative interviews exploring the behavior, knowledge, and attitudes of participants in the subculture (Ratner, 1993). The results of ethnographic studies are descriptive rather than statistical; they concentrate on environmental and social elements. They are particularly useful for studying emergent and little-understood phenomena and for learning more about hidden populations often omitted from nationally representative surveys. Ethnographic study is useful because it includes the meaning of events and actions of the participants.

Ethnographic research techniques permit researchers to enter a particular cultural setting and to observe and participate within it (Maher & Curtis, 1995). The tools of ethnographers, however, also limit the size of the sample of a population that can be studied. Crack users who frequent central locations and carry on alternative lifestyles within a Crackworld are far easier to identify than are those who are able to maintain a crack habit without resorting to the degradation of street life. A large-scale ethnographic study of sex-for-crack exchanges in seven major cities was funded by the National Institute on Drug Abuse and published with the title *Crack Pipe As Pimp* (Ratner, 1993). In it, the editor recommends the study of sex-for-crack exchanges in non-inner-city crack subcultures (p. 26).

To compare the crackworlds found in large metropolitan areas with the subculture that develops elsewhere calls for the tools of ethnography. Studies are needed which use qualitative interviews with long-term crack addicts whose habits have not been carried on in an inner-city area.

Interviews

To begin this broader study of Crackworld, a picture of the subculture as it has developed in a small, coastal city has been derived through interviews with crack-addicted prostitutes in 1994. This picture indicates that the characteristics of Crackworld transcend the lifestyles of urban addicts and extend to smaller cities and other areas. The implications of this subculture are far-reaching and transcend the patterns of social decay of the inner cities, extending to social decay in many different settings.

A study of the lifestyles of crack addicts in Daytona Beach, Florida, involved case studies of 17 long-term crack addicts. The focus of the study was "How do women support a crack cocaine habit?" It revealed the same issues and patterns found in previous studies of large urban areas.

The descriptions of Crackworld in the interviews in Daytona Beach parallel those described in studies of the lifestyles of crack addicts in decaying center cities of large metropolitan areas. Women interviewed in Daytona Beach, like those in Miami, Chicago, Harlem, San Francisco, Los Angeles, Denver, Philadelphia, and Newark all describe a lifestyle "totally organized around drug use" (Ratner, 1993, p. 19).

Table 1.1 describes the interviewees of Crackworld in Daytona Beach. Details outlined in the chart and the findings of many others have demonstrated some very strong patterns for women in Crackworld. Striking consistencies in crackworlds found throughout the country not only are symptoms of the social pathology in the subculture but also point to the causes of these disorders.

Findings

A summary of the findings[1] listed in Table 1.1 shows that although those interviewed were not from an inner-city crackworld, they, like women everywhere in Crackworld, all have much in common. Several commonalities are discussed below.

Onset at an Early Age. Many of those addicted to crack began substance abuse at an early age. Crack cocaine is often only one of many addictions in a lifetime of substance abuse. Many of the interviewees began a routine of dependency as teenagers. The problem goes far beyond the use of crack and begins with fundamentals. By focusing on crack addiction, treatment providers often miss the basis for the abuse of self, which often has a long-standing history.

One respondent said she had used drugs most of her life as "numb-erizers." She began drinking when she was 10 years old. She was introduced to crack when she was 23, at the time of the breakup of her marriage. She said that crack "took over."

Socioeconomic Factors. Some women can support their own habits and supply drugs for their male partners. A respondent described an early sexual relationship with a dealer that began with his supplying her with drugs when she was about 15. She said he used a pipe to control her. "He put a pipe in my mouth and I shut up. I wasn't going anywhere." When she and the "dope man" began smoking more than they were selling, her partner put her out on the street and told her not to come back until she got the money. She said, "It was never hard for me to get dope. I got lots and lots of drugs with or without sex."

Many long-term crack users have held legitimate jobs and consider themselves capable of supporting themselves and their children. None of them had ever held what is considered high-paying employment. Maintaining any kind of legitimate work for sustained periods in the crack lifestyle is virtually impossible. Women who can maintain a home have an advantage. They can charge smokers a small commission and support their habits without leaving home. Most addicts in Crackworld cannot support a home. Likewise, women have access to opportunities for transporting drugs if they can maintain a car, but most addicts sell their cars when they become desperate.

Most of the women in Crackworld depend on a man to supply their drugs. The market is violent and male dominated, and even women with means must negotiate for drugs. All the study participants' drug supplies depended on relationships with men as suppliers. Most of them also depended on men with whom they had intimate relationships for the essentials of living, such as food, housing, and clothing.

Relationships With Men. The lifestyle of crack addicts often involves relationships of dependency and domination by men who use access to drugs for control. Relationships with men as spouses or partners in Crackworld usually are negative. One participant commented, "It looks

TABLE 1.1 Comparison of Interviews

Respondent	Age at Interview	Nature of Addiction[a]	Environment of Use	Economics	Violence	Cheating	Sex Exchanges
1	31	18/Alcohol	at home "House"	Clerical/ sold crack/sex	Child abuse/ incest/rape	Steal from tricks	For money
2	28	10/Alcohol	"House"	Nurse's aide/ sold sex	Child abuse/ incest/rape/ domestic battery	Food stamp fraud	All types
3	28	13/Marijuana	"House"	Fast food/sex	Fear	No	All types
4	32	26/Crack	"House"	Male set up/ transport drugs	Child abuse/ incest/rape/ domestic battery/ suicide attempt	Food stamp fraud	Friends
5	36	29/Crack	At home/ outdoors	Male set up/ sold crack	Incest/domestic battery/fear	Stolen goods/ bad checks	All types
6	28	22/Cocaine	"House"/ anywhere	Male set up/ sold sex	Incest/rape/ domestic battery/ assault/fear/suicide attempt	Stole/robbed	All types
7	32	12/Various	Everywhere	Cook crack/ sold drugs/ male set up	Child abuse/ incest/rape/ attempted murder/ suicide attempt/fear	Armed robbery/ "jacking"/theft	All types
8	27	12/Marijuana	"Houses"	Posing as prostitute	Child abuse/rape	Steal from tricks	All types

9	27	Under 18/Various	At home	Sold drugs/male set up/drug transport	Child molesting/domestic battery/suicide attempt/fear	Sold fake dope	No
10	35	13/Various	Everywhere	Male set up/sold sex	Incest/rape/kidnap/fear	Steal from "tricks"	For money
11	35	15/Alcohol	At home	Maid/sell sex/food service/male set up	Domestic battery/rape/fear	Steal from "tricks"	For drugs/friends
12	27	13/Marijuana	At home	Mom, others set up/sold drugs	Date rape	"Do anything"	For money
13	21	13/Various	Vacant buildings/"houses"	Food service/retail/sold sex/drug transport	Rape/domestic battery/kidnap	1 time $10.00	All types
14	27	17/Alcohol	At home/"houses"/outdoors	Nurse's aide/housekeeping/stealing	Fear	Bad checks	"Chicken head"/all types
15	33	Over 21/Crack	Outdoors	Selling drugs/fronting/friends set up	Child abuse/domestic battery/fear	Shoplifting	No
16	32	15/Various	At home/car/motels	Sold/transport drugs/construction/m/f lovers set up	Rape/police brutality/assault	Steal from "tricks"/bad checks	For money
17	28	13/Alcohol	At home/motels	Housekeeping/nurse's aide/mate set up	Fear/suicide attempt	No	For money

a. Age at onset/first substance abused.

19

like I just bump into the wrong man, every time." Relationships with fathers and father figures often are negative as well. Few crack addicts report functional relationships in their families of origin. Most of them began a life of instability long before they began using crack.

After a lifetime of abuse of many kinds, one of the participants commented, "There's a lot of hatred in my heart." Another said, "I have a problem trusting men. I don't like taking money from men. I hated myself. I hated the men. All I felt was disgust."

One of the participants was a living example of the cycle of victimization. She was seriously abused in a series of foster homes when she was a small child, including both sexual and physical abuse. She was beaten by her husband. As a crack whore, she frequently was victimized by customers. Some beat her; others took her money or drugs.

Violence. Many females in Crackworld report experiences with violence among their earliest family recollections. Frequent violent episodes, along with threats and fear, are common to their lifestyle. Most female crack addicts have been the victims of violence. Many of them have been raped, sexually abused, and battered by intimates throughout their lives. In addition, many are raped by strangers.

Every one of the addicts interviewed mentioned instances of deep and intense fear of violence as part of the crack lifestyle.

An example is provided by one woman who, at age 36, has seen the violence in the drug market get worse. She said, "They didn't use to kill you, but nowadays they're actually taking lives . . . killing about space." She confided that she carried a razor blade or fingernail file for protection in Crackworld, but she did not carry a concealed weapon because "anytime the police stop you they will search you." She believed she needed protection because "Sometimes people flip out on you." "One guy threatened me with a knife," she said. According to her, "The best way to handle it is to 'talk them through it.' " She observed, "I was lucky that no one got physical with me. I have seen people lose their lives, both males and females."

This woman's luck ran out shortly after this interview.

She got a ride from a stranger who later dumped her out of the car and left her for dead in an old cemetery in the heart of the Crackworld section of Daytona Beach. She was hospitalized in critical care for weeks and convalesced slowly at home after that. She never recovered fully from the attack.

Prostitution. Most of the females in Crackworld exchange sexual services for money or for crack. The exchanges are various and depend on the needs of the moment. Some reported that they never exchanged sex for crack, but most admitted that in the desperation of craving, they might do anything.

The following graphic description gives one respondent's personal view of the crack whore's lifestyle.

> No morals, no principles. . . . I let them treat me like a dog. . . . I'm on my knees in the bathroom . . . there's an unbelievable stink. The water is off, but they still use it, and there is every kind of filth. When they open the door it smells bad. It gags you. And this disgusting guy pulls out his filthy, smelly dick, and I would suck it anyway.

Many do not make a practice of using condoms for sex. The threat of sexually transmitted diseases looms large in the subculture. In a world of disorganization and compulsion, the use of protection is unlikely. Feelings of degradation, guilt, and shame are common. In Crackworld, it is believed that women addicted to crack inevitably turn to using sex to get the drug. One participant explained, "AIDS was the last thing on my mind. I thought I was better off dead, anyway."

One of the participants was HIV positive. She became aware of her status in 1988, but so far she has not developed AIDS. She did not think that crack had been connected to contacting the HIV virus. She said, "I was always fast. I always had lots of boyfriends." She added, "All my life I have had problems with men, with getting rid of them."

Nonsexual Transactions. Many women are involved in nonsexual transactions within the crack market. Some sell drugs or transport them; some are used as decoys or messengers. Many women in Crackworld also are involved in acts of petty theft and cheating. For the most part, women participate only in nonviolent activities, but sometimes they are also involved in armed robberies and extortions.

One participant described her feelings as the lifestyle turned progressively more violent:

> At the end it got so bad . . . I was disoriented. I was violent, unliked, I caused shoot-outs. I was living a dead end. I realized it when a dear friend of mine was shot standing right next to me . . . after that I started going into "jacking" (armed robbery) in a serious way. I was the only woman. I intimidated them. I didn't give a damn. I'd set it up. They'd open the door to me, then the guys coming behind me would rob everybody.

This respondent's aggressive behavior was unique. The rest of the women interviewed used small-scale and personal illegitimate means to support addictions. A common target is a "trick" or "date" who pays for sexual services that are never received. As one participant put it, "I made a 'career' out of cheating 'Johns' out of their money."

Crack Houses. The general picture of crack houses in Daytona Beach that emerged from the descriptions in the interviews is an image of places of degradation. They are likely to be the homes of people who use and get crack for themselves by letting others smoke in their houses. Sometimes the owner can charge users a small fee for use of drugs and another fee for sex. The participants all agreed that there is always sex in crack houses.

A crack house may not have lights or water. Sometimes the place is not a residence but an abandoned or condemned and boarded up structure in which neighborhood users seek privacy. One participant described a typical crack house as follows: "No water, no lights, no food, NASTY! You are liable to get crabs, lice . . . a filthy place. It's a place for users who get out of hand."

According to the participants, it is not uncommon to find children in crack houses. They described abuse and neglect as common for these children. There is no doubt that crack houses are not healthy places for children or adults.

How Women Support a Crack Cocaine Habit. The environment of crack use is degrading and depraved, even when compared with other environments where substances are abused. The proportion of crack addicts who are women is larger than the proportion of heroin addicts previously reported to be female. As the proportion of addicted females using illegal drugs has increased, the roles for females in the subculture have become increasingly degrading. Women in Crackworld face an authoritarian subculture dominated and controlled by men. Control is imposed with fear and violence. Legitimate opportunities are limited within the lifestyle by addiction, and, for women, even illegitimate opportunities are limited by societal expectations for females.

Their own sexuality is the one resource most likely to be exploited by females in Crackworld. When women exchange sex for money or drugs, they re-create patterns begun early in their lives when they first experienced physical and sexual violation. Domination is based on violence; submission is coerced with fear. Relationships with men often are based on exploitation and objectification, and they promote dependency.

Illegitimate opportunities for women to support their need for crack often arise within the exploitative relationships with would-be sex partners. Finding themselves being used as objects, many women feel justified in taking advantage of and cheating their objectifiers. The resulting alienation, both personal and social, is a heavy price to pay for crack addiction.

One participant summed it up: "I feel like everything I done was wrong. Did you ever look in the mirror and you don't see nobody? Sometimes I think I was born just to suffer, to prove what pain is." The cost of dependency, victimization, and degradation of Crackworld is too great for women to support, by whatever means.

Case Study of a "Rock Star"

Life History of a "Rock Star"

Of the 17 women whose lives were studied for this text, one was chosen as an exemplar that provides a penetrating look at Crackworld. This woman's case was chosen because it contains many of the elements and patterns shown to be common among female crack users. In addition, as an intelligent and especially articulate subject, this woman provided depth and insight that bring the patterns and elements to life.

S. is a 28-year-old Native American woman who has smoked crack for more than 5 years. She has served more than 4 years in prisons in Georgia and Florida. A letter from S., written while she was in a treatment program in Largo Florida, was received in December, approximately 6 months after the interviews in the spring of 1993. According to the letter, since these interviews, S. had returned to street life and Crackworld, lost custody of her child, spent time in prison, and by the holiday season at the end of 1993, was making still another resolution to leave Crackworld behind.

Onset at an Early Age

S. was married to a drug dealer 3 months after her 15th birthday. At the time, she had smoked pot but not really been involved in other drugs. A few months after her marriage, she became addicted to Quaaludes. She also used various drugs from time to time, but she says, "Nothing got its grip on me before cocaine."

She was introduced to injecting cocaine when she was 22. She says, "After that I never stopped." A neighbor who was a street prostitute introduced her to smoking crack and showed her the ropes. As she said,

> "Smoke till you croak!" was my motto. 9- to 10-day binges were common. There was at least one 15-day binge. After that I had the coke bugs. I thought someone had sewn my eyelids shut. I heard the police in the air conditioning vent. I could feel my central nervous system deteriorating.

S. explained the symptoms of withdrawal from crack.

> They call it "Jonesing"—you're nervous, jumpy, dry mouth, eyes bothering you. You want no noise. You're pacing back and forth. There's just one thing on your mind. Have to have it! The crash is bad, mental pain. Mentally, I just couldn't ride it out.

Socioeconomic Factors

S. described "living from incident to incident." At the age of 22, S. worked as a bank clerk and made a decent salary. After she began to use crack heavily, she was unable to hold any job for long. She said, "This is a 'lifestyle.' When you are in it, there is no other topic. You live and breathe crack cocaine. It is the whole world. It took two months to lose everything to cocaine."

After that, S. prostituted and stole for what she needed. She found it hard to think about the ways she supported her habit. "The worst was beating a friend, demanding money, striking his car and then him, hitting him in the head with a high heel shoe, hurting him and threatening to rob him of money to buy crack."

According to S., joblessness is common in the crack subculture. "None of the women in crack have legitimate jobs. I tried that at first, but I lost them all in less than a month. I couldn't keep a job. I would be in the bathroom smoking, or I wouldn't go at all. Jobs interfered with my using."

In her second marriage, S. took up with another dealer called "Meatman." She explains his name:

> Years ago he was a down-and-out alcoholic who shoplifted meat to buy booze. Then he gave up the booze and started selling drugs. Later he would give the meat to the ones in the neighborhood who really needed it. They really liked him for that and so they still called him "Meatman," but it was a good name for him. He was the dope man, I was the "Rock Monster," or they call 'em "rock stars."

Dealers don't use. They are all about money. I saw what the money was one time on the beach at a motel during Spring Break. I saw my husband make $12,000 profit in 3 hours, and that was not all. After that I stopped counting.

Relationships With Men

S. was first molested by her father when she was about 7. She remembers,

He came into my bed one time during the night. It was never mentioned. But I knew that it happened . . . fondling. Shortly after that my brothers started experimenting, touching me. They were 4 and 5 years older than me. They knew better. For a long period, 2 to 3 years, they kept after me. It was bad enough that it led me to leave home at 14 to get away from them.

At 12 I was raped by a neighbor. I went over there to see my friend, but his dad was home alone, and he offered me a cigarette. I was taken in because I thought it was neat that he would let me smoke. Once he got me inside, he used intimidation to penetrate me.

My second husband beat me so much I lost count. He said he beat me to get me to stop using crack. I thought he just wanted me to stop because of the money. But he said it was for my own good. Afterward he would feel guilty, and then he gave me dope. It was crazy. . . . I saw him for what he really was for the way he treated addicts. He had a power trip over them, like little slaves to him. He would degrade them, treated them really bad, and they would beg him. . . . My husband was one of those who used crack to buy women.

Violence

S. described the crack subculture as extremely violent. She says,

I know of three women who are dead from robbing tricks. One got cracked in the head with a club, another got her eyes and tongue cut out. . . . About one or two out of five tricks turns into a rape with them taking sex without paying. I was punched, had my throat grabbed, my hair pulled.

Prostitution

S. explained sex-for-crack exchanges from her experiences.

In the beginning, crack stimulates sex. Later, men can't perform, and women get nothing, not even wet. But they have to do it to get crack. A woman who uses crack must prostitute or steal. She will turn a trick for $20—$15 if it comes to it, anything. She can find lots of tricks, no problem to find tricks, unless she's robbing, or "got something." Word gets around. If she robs some guy, she's going to be right back out there. It's just a matter of time and they will find her.

S. describes prostitution for crack whores.

At the bottom level of prostitution you have someone who will be on her knees in a crack house. She is dirty; has no regulars. Up from that you have someone who gets $10 to $20 for a trick, but she will exchange sex for dope, too. She is on the street. Higher you have prostitutes who make $50 to $100 for a trick. They have some regulars, but they are also out on the street picking up dates. Maybe they sit in the lounge of a hotel or somewhere.

S. admits that her own experiences with prostitution left her feeling degraded. She says, "I couldn't face what I had done, like I have done at least ten guys in a phone booth. To keep up the habit you need a lot of men with a lot of money." According to S.,

Blacks dominate, so whites get used and abused. They say, "Since white men used black women for ages, now we are going to get back" . . . like revenge. Dominating white women seems to give them a feeling of power. It's a euphoria. They "dog out the whites." White guys will pay a white woman $50 (for sex). But they will pay a black woman $10 for the same thing. Then, the black guys will sell crack cheaper to the black sisters.

S. did not insist on using condoms but had left it up to the buyer if he wanted to use one or not. She reports, "A lot more tricks are using rubbers. It depends on the guy."

Transactions

S. describes the crack market as male dominated.

I knew of three women in town who were female dealers. But in the crack life, women who sell carry guns. They have a man behind them, but silent. My husband would act as the supplier to some prostitutes. He fronted for them and they would sell out of motel rooms. Women were strictly pawns, consumers, and distributors, no more.

S. says, "Dealers can buy houses, cars, they can even retire. But sooner or later the cops will get something on them and they will lose it all. That's just the way it is.

Crack Houses

S. reports, "I've smoked anywhere. In houses, motels, parks, bathrooms at gas stations and fast food places, bathrooms everywhere, in the car at a red light, you name it." From her experiences, "A crack house is always really dirty. The water and lights are off . . . They are run by blacks. Once in a while there are whites using it more than blacks." S. repeats, as an afterthought, "Crack is a lifestyle."

NOTE

1. The interviewer was granted access by the staff and directors of a local drug treatment agency for women, the Anti-Recidivist Effort (ARE). She gained rapport with residents during volunteer work as the Parenting Program teacher for the treatment center.

The first few interviews were held in the interviewer's office in an academic setting for privacy. Later, it was found that, in order to avoid missed interviews and take advantage of flexible schedules, it was more efficient for the interviewer to stop by the treatment center on a routine basis. Staff members came to expect that the interviewer would come by and ask for a volunteer on Friday afternoons. Many residents were willing to participate. The research idea was explained to each respondent at the outset of the interview.

Some sessions lasted only a few hours; others continued through three or four sessions of several hours each. Interviewees preferred to hold the sessions in local parks. Most smoked cigarettes while they talked. Informal and pleasant surroundings enhanced the interviews. The interviewer took notes at the time of the meeting and reviewed the notes, adding details, immediately following the interview. As soon as possible, the notes were transcribed into complete descriptions and organized into six sections corresponding with the questions below.

The interviews covered the following questions, asked of each respondent.

1. What was the nature of your addiction?
2. What was the environment of your use?
3. What were the economics of your crack use?
4. What (if any) types of violence did you experience?
5. What kinds of cheating (if any) did you carry out?
6. In what ways (if any) were you involved with selling sexual services?

2. Criminalization
of Pregnancy

Because the use of condoms is not likely in the desperate and degrading sexual activities carried on in Crackworld, the risk of pregnancy is high. Many crack addicts become pregnant, but few men, customers, or addict sex partners feel responsible for the children produced in these exchanges. "Crack babies" became the subject of a great deal of public interest in 1989. A public alarm was sounded about "crack babies," "cocaine babies," or "snow babies" who were born addicted and physically defective. Many articles and research reports have been published about the problems of infants born to crack-abusing mothers. The infants born of crack unions come into the least fortuitous circumstances. They are likely to suffer from various risk factors in addition to their parents' drug habits.

The Criminalization of Pregnancy:
Concepts and Issues

Born Hooked

It is clear that there are many problems likely to arise when crack addicts become pregnant. Of urban drug abusers enrolled in prenatal care, cocaine users were significantly less likely than other users to be married and were less well nourished. Cocaine users reported significantly more sexually transmitted diseases, prior low birth weight infants, spontaneous and elective abortions, and greater use of alcohol, cigarettes, marijuana, opiates, and other illicit drugs during pregnancy. With so many risk factors, it is difficult to isolate the independent risk for adverse neonatal outcomes caused by cocaine use during pregnancy (Frank et al., 1988). Results of some research suggest that babies born to mothers addicted to cocaine were damaged more by their environment than by any effect of the drug ("Cocaine Babies," 1991). Available research on drug-exposed infants shows a mix of findings. The effects of prenatal cocaine exposure have not been isolated (Myers, Olson, & Kaltenback, 1992).

Many researchers have shown that the problems posed by crack addiction and pregnancy are significant (Zuckerman et al., 1989). An estimate that there are at least 375,000 babies born in the United States each year affected by their mother's cocaine use was widely reported before 1990 (Fallon, 1990). By 1992, the estimate had shifted to more than 400,000 crack-exposed infants born annually in the United States (Metsch, McCoy, & Weatherby, 1996). A special hearing of the congressional committee on Children, Youth, and Families in April of 1989, called "Born Hooked: Confronting the Impact of Perinatal Substance Abuse," was devoted to the subject. Crack cocaine was called an "epidemic" and a "scourge," with women and children as the casualties. According to the congressional survey, substance abuse has a devastating impact on the nation's most vulnerable citizens. Although the number of drug-exposed babies remains relatively small, they are among the most expensive babies to care for. These children have the ability to swamp every system involved with their care, including hospitals, child protective services, foster care, and schools. The problems these children face "are the tragic effect of a decade of national neglect" (Miller, 1989).

The Criminalization of Cocaine

Legislative control over dangerous drugs can be dated from attempts in the 19th century to prevent acute poisoning. Consumers called for regulations about labeling certain substances that might be purchased in ignorance of their lethal potential or might be too easily available for suicide. At that time, Americans received opium and morphine from their physicians for pain relief, and they also bought whatever they wanted over the counter or from mail-order catalogues. Consumption of opium in the United States rose steadily before and after the Civil War.

The Pure Food and Drug Act of 1906 provided for the most common concern of consumers, correct labeling. Any "patent medicine" had to reveal on the label whether it included morphine, cocaine, cannabis, or chloral hydrate. It simply informed the purchaser whether any of these drugs were present; it did not prevent purchase or restrict the amount of the drug (Musto, 1991).

The Harrison Act of 1914 demonstrated that Congress wanted to control drug use. In 1919, the intent of reformers behind the law was achieved. Maintenance of addicts on prescriptions for narcotics was outlawed, and the federal government could take action nationwide to arrest and convict health professionals who practiced maintenance of narcotic-addicted patients. Those who had been addicted to the out-lawed substances became criminals. This "no maintenance" policy toward narcotics was applied to alcohol only a few months later, when the Volstead Act made drinking alcoholic beverages illegal and imposed criminal penalties.

Cocaine was introduced in the 1880s as a "wonder substance." It was praised by physicians for its ability to counteract melancholy, which now is called depression. Cocaine was made readily available to sniff as a treatment for sinusitis or hay fever. It also was available in soft drinks such as Coca-Cola until 1900. Because of cocaine's association with violence, paranoia, and collapsed careers, proposals for laws against its use became popular by 1910. By the 1930s, the use of cocaine had decreased (Musto, 1991).

In the 1980s, one hundred years after the introduction of cocaine in the United States, the country appeared to be in another era of widespread use. Conditions were similar to those that had prevailed around 1900, before the onslaught against drug use led to a substantial reduction in the use of opiates, heroin, cocaine, and alcohol. At that earlier time, there was widespread fear and intolerance, along with dire predictions about the future destructive potential of cocaine on U.S.

society. That such a national response could occur then must make us pause now before making any predictions about the future impact of cocaine in the United States (Musto, 1991).

The Crack Cocaine Crisis

The crack cocaine crisis was recognized formally in the summer of 1986. It was defined as a "crisis" by the House of Representatives, Select Committee on Narcotics Abuse and Control and Select Committee on Children, Youth, and Families. Their hearings necessarily had political overtones because it was an election year. To add fuel to the furor, the death of a well-known athlete, Len Bias, was attributed to crack in the media blitz following his ill-explained demise. Crack became the most important story of the year, and Congress responded quickly with the 1986 Narcotics Penalties and Enforcement Act.

The law was passed hastily, without much study of its impact. No surveys were made, and all those who testified before the committee represented "the extent of crack use in the U.S., the serious health consequences it presents to those who abuse it, and the law enforcement problems crack is creating" (Rangel, 1986, p. 91). In his opening statement to the joint select committee hearing on "The Crack Cocaine Crisis," the Honorable Charles Rangel made the following recommendation:

> Cocaine is threatening the vitality of the generation of Americans we are counting on to lead us into the 21st century. . . . [T]he crack epidemic [is] part of the overall cocaine abuse problem in America. This problem will continue as long as . . . the Administration and State Department view the international drug problem as "business as usual." Only when we give the drug problem the foreign policy priority it deserves will we ever begin to get a handle on the cocaine crisis sweeping our nation. (Rangel, 1986, p. 93)

The focus of the Joint Committee's report was on the street market. The real concern was crack-related violence in inner cities. In their concern for stopping violence, the committee failed to address the larger issues behind the violence in the crack market. The large-scale, international links to financial institutions were forgotten in the furor about crack in the street.

As a result of the "get tough" approach introduced in 1986, cocaine retailers who sell crack are punished severely, whereas cocaine wholesalers who sell large quantities of cocaine powder are treated relatively leniently. According to United States Sentencing Guidelines (§2D.1.1), a dealer convicted for selling 5 grams of crack and a dealer convicted for selling 500 grams of cocaine are both to be sentenced to 5 years imprisonment. That is a disparity of 100 to 1. The stiff mandatory minimum penalties were said to send a message to crack dealers, who were characterized as "super bad guys" (Wilkins, 1993).

Concern continues to revolve around the extremes of violence found in the street trade of crack. The focus on crack not only distracts interest from the international drug trade but also takes attention away from the multiple socioeconomic problems leading to that violence. Mandatory minimum sentencing laws were a "quick fix." In their application, these laws were extremely discriminatory (Wilkins, 1993). Although in theory the laws were color blind, in effect they become extremely racially biased. More than 90% of crack offenders are black (*U.S. v. Dumas*, 1995).

Racial differences exist in the lifestyles of black and white crack users and in the influences they face. Whites have less need to commit crimes in order to pay for expenses. African Americans are more likely to turn to crime to cover expenses. Differences that appear to be racial are in many cases actually socioeconomic. The degree of access to other income and the likelihood of living in an environment of high rates of drug use and crime are important factors influencing lifestyle. Inciardi and his associates (Inciardi, Pottieger, & Surrat, 1996) found that race-specific explanations of crime and crack are likely to obscure the role that social and environmental factors play in the overall epidemiology of crack use. Current forecasts of crack use estimate that more than half of all users are white, but according to one report, "no white person has ever been convicted of a crack offense in the federal courts of Boston, Denver, Chicago, Los Angeles, Miami or Dallas" (Morley, 1995).

There are two reasons why this law, which may have been motivated by concerns about violence that were not strictly racist, has become a tool used against black street users and dealers of crack. On one hand, as long as the law enforcement focus is maintained at a lower level, the higher levels are not affected. The drug trade has a pyramidal structure, and those few at the top are not disturbed when the focus is on crack retailers. The vast sums of money flowing into financial institutions from the international drug trade remain secure. The status quo of those with wealth and means remains unaffected as long as the efforts to stop drug problems are expended in a "war on crack" in the streets. Politicians can continue to call for harsh and stringent measures as long as the measures are applied only in violation of the civil rights of citizens of inner cities and low-income areas, who are largely powerless in the political arena.

On an even more pragmatic level, the focus of criminal action on street dealers and users of crack is the decision of prosecutors. Prosecutors ultimately are responsible for all criminal charges. They set policy for law enforcement, decide to develop or drop cases, and provide instructions to juries. Prosecutors may decide to go after the street trade because of its easy access. The outcome is likely to produce many negotiated pleas and large numbers of convictions to the prosecutors' credit. If prosecutors decide to take on the drug organization at a higher level, they are likely to find that drug wholesalers are far outside their jurisdiction. Building a case against any extensive organization implies search warrants, accountants, informants, and long, involved investigations. Strictly from pragmatics, it is likely that prosecutors will continue to pursue those who are most vulnerable.

The strict prosecution of crack dealers and users that began in 1986 has resulted in a large population of black inner-city residents being held in the jails and prisons of the United States. Among the prisoners in federal and state correctional facilities in 1993, 48% were black, 45% were white (including Hispanic), approximately 1% were other races, and the remaining 6% were unknown—both black and white (Maguire & Pastore, 1994). Because black people account for less than 15% of the population in the United States, their large numbers in state and federal prisons show the result of focusing law enforcement efforts on black communities. The result has been intense police activity with little change for the better in inner-city neighborhoods.

In 1973, the rate of incarceration was 97 per 100,000, and by 1993 the rate had risen to 350 of every 100,000 persons in the population of the United States being held in a state or federal prison (Maguire & Pastore, 1994). The nation's imprisonment rate is considered one of the highest in the world. In 1995, 9 years after the harsh drug sentencing guidelines went into effect, the Sentencing Guidelines Commission found even more deadly violence on the streets.

A surge of violent juvenile crime has coincided with the increase in drug arrests, particularly among nonwhites in urban areas. A National Institute of Justice study in 1995 found that juvenile drug arrests began to increase sharply for nonwhites in 1985, following a 10-year decline that began in 1975. This increase reflected, in part, the degree to which drug enforcement had focused on street drug markets, more often involving black drug dealers. The number of arrests rose again, from approximately 200 per 100,000 in 1985 to twice that number 5 years later. Drug arrests for white youths declined, in part because of a policy shift away from marijuana arrests.

Arresting more African Americans and locking up adult dealers may have contributed to the increased recruitment of juveniles into the drug trade. Dealer/users usually are recruited to the drug market from the ranks of unemployed, inner-city youth (Blumstein, 1995). In 1992, after 7 years of enforcement of strict treatment and mandatory minimum sentences for crack dealer/users by the United States courts, there were no signs that street violence was abating. In fact, the number of homicides committed by young people, the number of homicides they committed with guns, and the arrest rate for nonwhite juveniles for drug offenses doubled.

Street drug markets became increasingly violent, and dealer/users became even younger in the 1990s. When juveniles are recruited to sell crack, they arm themselves with guns, and juvenile use of firearms is more random and reckless than that of adults. A gun is seen as effective protection for juveniles transporting valuable merchandise. Those not in the drug trade also believe that a gun can provide protection, as well as status and power. As more people feel threatened by the firearms around them, they also are more likely to obtain guns. The increase in violence is linked to the diffusion of guns into the hands of juveniles and to the general community, a result of the growth in numbers of youths in the illegal drug trade and the illegal arms trade (Blumstein, 1995).

Despite the lack of evidence of a decline in violence to support "get tough" laws against drug dealers, popular opinion has grown in support of "mandatory minimum" sentences for drug users as well as dealers (Maguire & Pastore, 1994). In 1993, the Federal Sentencing Commission began hearings on crack cocaine and the impact and outcome of stricter penalties for crack use. Testimony showed that links between crack and violence are socioeconomic and systemic. Law enforcement measures to combat violence that are aimed at lower levels and individuals are costly and not effective (Wilkins, 1993). In 1995, the commission voted unanimously against the disparity in sentences for crack and cocaine offenders and recommended new guidelines. Congress and President Clinton rejected their recommendation before it could become law. It was the first time that any recommendation by the Sentencing Commission ever had been rejected. Mandatory minimum sentences have had a racist impact and will likely lead to strong conflicts in the years to come.

Congress and President Clinton's support of mandatory minimum sentences for crack dealer/users shows their concern about public fear, even if that fear is the result of political and media hype. The direct relationship between crack and other crimes has not been confirmed by empirical data; the relationship is an indirect one based on broader socioeconomic causes. Instead of reporting that crack causes crime, it may be more valid to say that crack and crime cause each other, or that crack and crime have the same causes, or even that crack and crime are the result of multiple causes, and they in turn set off multiple effects.

The crack-crime connection is an interrelationship: The lifestyle of Crackworld reinforces crime. From the perspective of youth, all the dangers associated with potential death, overdose, arrest, and street violence are welcomed as intoxicating challenges. The elevated levels of violence associated with competition among traffickers for control of given markets has become systemic. Violence against otherwise law-abiding crack-using citizens over debts or cheating is routine (McBride & Rivers, 1996).

Continuing to focus efforts against drug addiction on crack street dealer/users is clearly racist. Even though this may not have been the intent of those who formulated the policy, the evidence that has accumulated is clear. The relationship between drugs and crime must be considered in the context in which drugs are used and crime occurs. Ridding inner cities of crack dealers will neither solve the problems found there nor eliminate the social ills that cause the violence perpetrated there.

Crack Babies

Most studies show that mothers who use cocaine have babies with smaller neonatal head circumferences and impaired fetal growth (Chasnoff, 1989a, 1989b). Marijuana has similar consequences for babies. The use of cigarettes and alcohol adds to the amount of impairment. Any interventions aimed at stemming infant mortality must take a comprehensive approach to the risks involved (Zuckerman et al., 1989).

The criminalization of substance abuse by pregnant women is one intervention for which the strongest impact is on black crack mothers. Other pregnant substance abusers are likely to be treated as "sick" rather than "criminal." Despite the relatively higher risk of fetal alcohol syndrome occurring in newborn infants, there have been no notorious cases of women charged with crimes because of it. Alcohol abuse during pregnancy is not generally considered criminal, even though fetal alcohol syndrome is responsible for many of the same types of birth anomalies found in infants with crack-related defects. The image of depraved "rock monsters" overburdening social services systems and producing countless defective children was much more threatening in the media than the image of a pregnant alcoholic or a pregnant woman using tranquilizers. The pictures shown to the nation were of black women, and they were meant to instill fear. Once again, political motives predominated—the concern was not for the babies. Many more babies are born affected by their mother's exposure to hazardous living and working conditions than are born affected by exposure to cocaine.

Nor was the concern for the addicted mothers, many of whom are negatively affected by multiple personal and social problems outside their addictions to crack. Instead, building public concern for "crack babies" created a demonic stereotype of a "crack mother." She was pictured as a mother with lack of concern for her infant and lack of self-control. As an unfit mother, the pregnant crack addict was outside criminal and moral bounds. She was much more likely to face censure than a pregnant alcoholic or even a pregnant woman who ingests powdered cocaine through her nose.

It is important to consider the problem of pregnant cocaine users from several perspectives, not simply from that of fear. According to some estimates, more than 5 million women of childbearing age use an illicit drug, many of them using more than one substance. Almost 1 million use cocaine. An estimated 3.8 million young women use marijuana. There are almost 6 million women in the United States who abuse alcohol. Some estimate that more than 20% of women in the United States smoke cigarettes. According to at least one survey of pregnant women, 15% tested positive for substance abuse (U.S. House of Representatives, 1990).

In order to have a reliable estimate of the number of crack babies being born, some evidence must be assumed to be an indication that an infant has been negatively affected by crack. One of the most common indicators used to show that an infant is a "crack baby," in addition to his or her mother's use of crack, is low birth weight. The proportion of low birth weight babies increased in 1991. Seven percent of all infants and nearly 17% of black infants were low birth weight babies, the highest rates since 1978. Lack of prenatal care combined with an increased rate of births to teenagers and unmarried women are two of the factors related to low birth weight. Many of the mothers subject to these factors are poor. Every day, according to the Children's Defense Fund, 2,685 babies are born into poverty, 638 are born to mothers who receive no, or late, prenatal care, and 742 are born with low birth weight ("Prior Priority," 1991).

Compared with other industrialized countries, the United States has the dubious distinction of ranking 22nd in the proportion of infants who will die before their first birthday and 31st in the proportion of low birth weight babies. It costs more than $1,500 per day to keep a low birth weight baby in intensive care, compared with a total of $500 per woman for prenatal care. It is likely that as many as 25% of women receive late prenatal care or none at all, the highest proportion in nearly 20 years. More than 8.5 million women have no health insurance (Bagley & Merlo, 1995).

Although having a crack-abusing mother certainly is a problem, the magnitude of other problems faced by infants in the lowest socioeconomic levels of the United States is much greater. The high rates of infant mortality and low birth weight babies born in the United States are both a symptom and a result of the quality of life in U.S. society. On one hand, the large number of infants who die or who are born with poor chances for the future shows a lack of public concern for babies whose lives are actually threatened more by the lack of preventive and supportive services than by crack addiction. On the other hand, these indicators of low quality of life show the reality of the underclass.

The costs of birth into a life of squalor for a newborn child are not measurable. Instead, a simple dimension of the problem must be measured if a single cause is to be found and public interest captured. When costs are being estimated by the media or political surveys, complex issues seldom are addressed. The analysts have chosen crack as the single cause to be measured, and the costs of crack addiction in the lives of infants is projected.

Various estimates have been used to project the cost of crack babies. Caring for newborn infants whose mothers used crack during their pregnancy is estimated to have added more than $500 million a year nationally to the costs of normal labor, delivery, and newborn care in 1990 (Scott, 1991). Cocaine-exposed infants require hospitalizations that average 4 days longer and cost $2,610 more than nonexposed babies. Cocaine-exposed infants are 50% more likely than nonexposed infants to require intensive care and more than twice as likely to have a low birth weight ("Cocaine-Exposed Babies," 1991). The validity of these estimates has not been questioned, even though the mothers' crack use was only one of many risk factors likely to have been involved in the reported labor and delivery problems.

Estimates of costs of infant mortality and morbidity have had no observable effect on public policy. In the state of Florida, for example, the cost for infants born with problems resulting from cocaine is estimated to be about $8,179 per baby. Of the current expenditures, 11.8% is for prevention, compared with 82.2% for medical care after the baby is born.

Analysis of Judicial Alternatives

Criminalization

A large number of criminal actions against cocaine-abusing pregnant women originate in Florida, reflecting a punitive approach to crack mothers. There are more pregnant women in prison in Florida than in any other state, and a number of babies are born while their mothers are incarcerated in the state (Maguire & Pastore, 1994).

Criminally prosecuting mothers who give birth to drug-dependent babies conflicts with the stated public policy underlying Florida's child welfare laws. The Florida legislature's paramount concern in providing comprehensive protective services for abused and neglected children is supposed to be "to preserve the family life of the parent and children, to the maximum extent possible, by enhancing the parental capacity for adequate child care." Instead, enforcing a punitive policy actually results in lower parental capacity to provide for adequate child care. Criminal prosecutions needlessly destroy the family by incarcerating the mother when alternative measures could both protect the child and stabilize the family (Spitzer, 1987).

This contradiction between goals and application of one state's policy on pregnant substance abusers is typical. Discrepancies among policies, legislation, and case law concerning crack babies in many states resulted from public confusion and hasty responses that accompanied the fear of the crack epidemic spreading across the United States in the late 1980s.

Public policy, procedure, and laws designed to control women who use drugs during their pregnancy can be classified into three types: narcotics laws, criminalization laws, and informant laws. All three types of law focus on punishing a mother for drug use so that the fetus will be protected.

Narcotics laws apply existing prohibitions against drug possession and distribution to pregnant women. Both men and women lose their liberty when they are convicted for illegal drug use; pregnant women may lose their liberty for longer. The intent of existing narcotics laws has been expanded so that women can be charged with delivering a controlled substance to a minor when the recipient is a fetus or newborn infant.

Criminalization laws are recently drafted statutes that specifically define behaviors such as fetal endangerment or fetal abuse. Many authors have called this fetal abuse path in policy a legal "slippery slope" (Bagley & Merlo, 1995). Fetal abuse laws have two important limitations. They define a fetus as a child, but court decisions have not supported the concept of a fetus as a separate entity. They also hold the rights of a fetus as above the rights of a pregnant woman to make decisions about her own body.

Informant laws are those most often used to take away the rights of the mother. Informant laws require health care workers or other treatment providers to report suspected or actual drug use by pregnant women. Women who are routinely subjected to drug testing or the testing of their newborns are likely to be poor and either black or Hispanic.

Fetal Abuse As Child Abuse

When pregnant mothers are charged with "child abuse" before their babies have been born, there may be some question about how the behavior is defined in the law. In most statutes, reference is made to nonaccidental harm inflicted on children by those responsible for their care. Three issues arise from these statutes: the meaning of "nonaccidental," the proof of harm, and whether fetuses are to be considered as children.

Child abuse laws are enacted at the state level. Their purpose is to protect infants and children from abuse and neglect perpetrated by parents or guardians. When someone reports to a state's division of child protective services that a child is being abused or neglected, a worker usually will conduct a preliminary investigation. If abuse or neglect is substantiated, the worker may petition the court for temporary custody of the child.

In many states, child protective service agencies have petitioned the courts in order to get protective custody of fetuses. In these actions, it has been affirmed that the child (fetus) is or will be abused or neglected. The Supreme Court, however, upheld that for state child protection laws to apply to the unborn fetus, the laws must specifically define a "fetus" as a "child," or it must be clear that the state legislature intended an unborn fetus to be considered a child under the child abuse and neglect laws (*Webster v. Reproductive Health Services*, 1989).

Some state divisions of child protective services have tried to obtain protective custody of a fetus in order to get custody of the child upon birth. New Jersey enacted a child protection statute that is applicable to an unborn fetus. The statute provides,

> Whenever it shall appear that any child within this state is of such circumstances that his welfare will be endangered unless proper care or custody is

provided, an application *may be filed* seeking that the Bureau of Children's Services accept and provide such care or custody of such child as the circumstances may require. The provisions of this section shall be deemed to include an application on behalf of an unborn child. (NJ Stat. Ann. §30:4C-11)

When a charge of improper parenting or delivery of a controlled substance is based on using illicit substances while pregnant, the question that must be addressed by the court is whether fetal abuse is child abuse. Most states do not recognize fetal abuse as child abuse (Kantrowitz, 1989). The following is Florida's statute (1993) with regard to child abuse; many states have similar statutes.

Whoever, willfully or by culpable negligence, deprives a child of, or allows a child to be deprived of, necessary food, clothing, shelter, or medical treatment, or who, knowingly or by culpable negligence, permits physical or mental injury to a child, and in so doing causes great bodily harm, permanent disability, or permanent disfigurement to such child, shall be guilty of a felony of the third degree. (Sec. 827.04(1))

At the district level, some courts of appeal have held that a child abuse statute does not include a fetus and, therefore, that the defendant cannot be prosecuted for child abuse based on introduction of drugs into her own body during gestation (*State v. Gethers*, 1991). A New York City court also held that a defendant cannot be charged with endangering the welfare of a child based on acts that endanger the unborn (*The People of the State of New York v. Melissa A. Morabito*, 1992). The Kentucky Supreme Court decided that the offense of criminal child abuse does not extend to the defendant's use of drugs while pregnant (*Commonwealth v. Welch*, 1993).

Many cases of drug-exposed and drug-addicted infants reach the dependency side of the juvenile court. The first point of entry of drug-exposed infants and their families into the juvenile court system is often immediately after birth. Many hospitals routinely perform neonatal toxicology screens when maternal substance abuse is suspected. Based on a positive toxicology test, the hospital may report the results to the child protective services agency, which in turn may ask the juvenile court to prevent the child's release to the parents while an investigation takes place. Child neglect is an issue with "boarder babies" being abandoned by their parents. Crack addiction is said to have led to the creation of a large number of babies being boarded in maternity, pediatric, and other settings because they have been abandoned by, or taken away from, their parents (Levy & Rutter, 1992). Babies being abandoned may be directly related to threats of civil and criminal action and to fear of authorities on the part of childbearing addicts. Threat of court action against pregnant drug users also may be indirectly responsible for harm inflicted from unprofessional abortions and lack of adequate care during pregnancy.

Courts have ruled that the use of drugs during pregnancy is by itself sufficient basis to trigger a child-abuse report and to support juvenile court dependency jurisdiction (Sagatun, 1993).

Such cases, however, seldom are upheld on appeal. For example, the Court of Appeals of Ohio decided that the juvenile court has no jurisdiction to regulate the conduct of a pregnant adult for the purpose of protecting the health of her unborn child (*Cox v. Court of Common Pleas*, 1988).

Although the state may justify coercion of cocaine mothers on the basis of its interest in protecting the fetus, it does not undertake any duty to ensure the necessary care for the woman's body. Instead, when pregnant addicts are handled by the court, the duty for protecting the fetus is imposed entirely on the pregnant woman. A wide variety of acts or conditions on the part of a pregnant woman could pose some threat to her fetus, including failure to eat well; using nonprescription, prescription, or illegal drugs; engaging in sexual intercourse; exercising or not exercising; smoking; drinking alcohol; and even ingesting something as common as caffeine. Other threats, such as physical harm resulting from accident or disease and working or living near toxic substances, also are significant when it comes to imposing responsibility (Kasinsky, 1993).

Harm and danger to a potential life may be greatest from an environment over which the mother has little control. The perils of pollution and ecological damage to unborn children, which are the responsibility of the state, remain unconsidered in child abuse and neglect issues (Mariner, Glantz, & Annas, 1990).

These environmental risks are likely to be high for those pregnant women who also are at the greatest risk of being criminalized for substance abuse.

Delivery of a Controlled Substance to a Minor

Women can be charged with delivery of a controlled substance to a minor when blood test results are positive for cocaine at the moment of birth. This action presumes that health care personnel will provide information and that the mother has no right to privacy. The state can require a physician to administer a toxicology test to a pregnant woman without her consent if there is a compelling interest that outweighs her Fourth Amendment right to privacy from government intrusion. The state statute, however, must be strictly worded for the protection of infant rights over the rights of the mother (Appel, 1992).

The state of Missouri has one such strictly worded statute. Its wording includes the following:

> [N]eglect also includes prenatal exposure to a controlled substance . . . used by the mother for a non-medical purpose, as evidenced by withdrawal symptoms in the child at birth, results of a toxicology test performed on the mother at delivery or the child at birth, or medical effects or developmental delays during the child's first year of life that medically indicate prenatal exposure to a controlled substance.

In addition, any

> person with responsibility for the care of children, [who] has reasonable cause to suspect that a child has been or may be subjected to conditions or circumstances which would reasonably result in abuse or neglect, including the use of a controlled substance by a pregnant woman for a non-medical purpose, . . . shall immediately report or cause a report to be made to the Missouri division of family services. (Missouri Senate Bill No. 756, 1990)

Many medical and legal experts criticize the practice of administering toxicology tests to nonconsenting pregnant women. These experts believe that toxicology tests given without the knowledge or consent of the patient violate their professional trust (Appel, 1992). Such tests raise the issues of discrimination, consent, and confidentiality. They often target women who cannot afford prenatal care or who can afford only to go to public hospitals or clinics. These women are labeled "high risk" and are tested routinely without their consent. Those who can afford private care remain effectively insulated from this form of state intrusion (Robin-Vergeer, 1990).

Hair analysis also has been used in some studies to detect gestational cocaine exposure. Samples of hair are collected from the mothers, and meconium, urine, and hair are also collected from newborns ("Best Way," 1992; Marques, Tippetts, & Branch, 199). Intrusiveness and right to privacy issues are important with hair analysis, as with urine and blood testing.

Florida, along with many other states, passed a statute in 1987 calling for state intervention when infants are born drug dependent. It was argued that although legislators may not have the right to protect the unborn, they must make an effort to protect the quality of life for children born to drug-dependent mothers. Hospital workers are required to notify the state department of Health and Rehabilitative Services immediately whenever babies are born with drugs in their systems. Child dependency proceedings can then be initiated to remove the child from parental custody (Spitzer, 1987). Throughout the United States, special prosecutors handling child abuse cases have made it clear that no woman, whether she is pregnant or not, has the right to use cocaine. In this area, they see no reason for concern about legal rights (Curriden, 1990).

Jennifer Johnson was the first woman in the United States to be convicted for delivery of a controlled substance to a minor on the birth of a baby with traces of cocaine in her system. The Florida Supreme Court did not uphold the conviction. (A case study follows later in the chapter.)

Likewise, the circuit court in Michigan held that the use of cocaine by pregnant women, which may result in postpartum transfer of cocaine through the umbilical cord to their infants, is not the type of conduct that the legislature intended to be prosecuted under the *delivery of cocaine* statutes (*People v. Hardy*, 1991).

The court decisions are, no doubt, a reaction to the obvious limits of the criminal approach to the problem of cocaine pregnancies. In order to have proof of delivery of a controlled substance to the newborn child, the child must be born alive. In addition, evidence of delivery of cocaine must rest on blood tests done at the moment of birth. Positive results indicate cocaine use very close to the delivery. There is no way to prove delivery of cocaine to the fetus in the first or second trimester of pregnancy, although the damage to the developing child from drug use may be great during the early stages and long before the moment of birth.

Medical personnel may avoid reporting cocaine use by pregnant women because they believe that, out of fear of prosecution, mothers will stay away from prenatal care (Mills & Bishop, 1990). Some prosecutors disagree. Those who favor criminal sanctions say that the fear of pregnant addicts avoiding prenatal care is not a sufficient concern to interfere with the action of the state to protect the unborn. From this perspective, if laws against crack mothers should not be enforced because they might keep pregnant addicts from seeking prenatal care, then child abuse laws should not be enforced either. Child abuse penalties may deter parents from obtaining medical care for abused children out of fear of criminal consequences in the same ways that crack abuse penalties may deter mothers from seeking medical care for themselves while pregnant (Logli, 1990).

Although the state's motive in prosecuting pregnant women may be to provide an incentive for them to stop using drugs, drug treatment is largely unavailable to them. Their pregnancy acts as a disqualifying factor for most programs (Kasinsky, 1993).

Manslaughter

Pregnant drug users may be charged with manslaughter even though the statutes were intended for third party criminal culpability. For example, the Florida criminal code makes the willful killing of an unborn quick child, by any injury *to the mother* of such child that would be murder if it resulted in the death of such mother, to be deemed manslaughter, a felony in the second degree (Florida Criminal Code 782.09, 1992). The law does not mention injury done *by the mother* to herself, yet there have been cases after the second trimester in which infants were stillborn and their mothers were charged with manslaughter. The court must decide that the death resulted from cocaine use for a crack mother to be convicted of manslaughter.

Attributing the stillbirth of an infant to cocaine abuse and considering this to be manslaughter comes from a "reasonable person" perspective about the law. The rationale behind this approach is that pregnant women are being asked only to act reasonably. If a woman elects to have unprotected sex, and once pregnant elects not to have an abortion, she takes on the additional responsibilities to see that, as far as possible, the child will be born healthy (Curriden, 1990). This may not seem so reasonable to a pregnant crack user.

The pregnant addict may not realize that she is pregnant until far into the first trimester and after significant risk of damage to the fetus already has been incurred. She may expect that if she uses cocaine, she is likely to have a spontaneous abortion. Although the numbers of spontaneous miscarriages among cocaine-abusing pregnant women are high, using the drug may not bring about the results she sought, and instead an unhealthy infant may result.

Finally, holding responsible for the healthy birth of the child the pregnant mother who carries her fetus to full term, rather than electing to have an abortion, assumes that safe, no-cost abortions are available to all women in the first few weeks of pregnancy. Legal, medically authorized abortions are not free to any female who wants to have one. Adequate prenatal health care is not easily available to all pregnant women, either. Without them, pregnant addicts in the throes of a lifestyle of compulsion are not likely to take care of their own health and well-being or to be responsible for that of their unborn children.

It is doubtful whether manslaughter charges would ever result in a conviction for a cocaine mother if tested in a jury trial. It is even more unlikely that the charge would be upheld in an appeal to a higher court. The case law is clear: The legal conception of "person" does not include a fetus (Spitzer, 1987). The Supreme Court has held that at no state of development is a fetus a "person" with legal rights separate from those of the mother (Paltrow, 1990). When cocaine mothers have been convicted of manslaughter, it was the result of their guilty pleas without the deliberation of public trials.

Involuntary Detention

Punishment, rehabilitation, and deterrence all have been used to justify involuntary detention of pregnant addicts, along with education and protection for the "infant" (Mills & Bishop, 1990). For some, detention is the key element in treating pregnant cocaine addicts to reduce the severity of the effects of cocaine use on the fetus (New York Senate Committee on Investigations, Taxation and Government Operations, 1989). According to *The New York Times*, when medical doctors who were maternal-fetal specialists were surveyed in 1986, more than half of them agreed that pregnant women who refuse medical advice and endanger the life of the fetus should be detained in hospitals and forced to follow their physicians' orders (Lewin, 1987). Some law enforcement agents and state prosecutors have justified the detention of pregnant cocaine addicts in jails and lock-up facilities for this reason, not necessarily because of punishment or retributive goals.

In effect, the state has taken custody of a child before it is born (Gest, 1989). In other words, the mother-fetus relationship can cause conflict because the treatment of one involves the mistreatment of the other. There is an understood obligation to the mother's health and well-being, but with involuntary detention, the health and well-being of the fetus comes first, although this is not a legally recognized obligation (Nelson & Milliken, 1988).

Some public officials and researchers have suggested that drug users can be civilly committed to a drug treatment program while they are pregnant. Involuntary civil commitment is a process whereby an individual is found to pose a danger to herself or others and is forced to undergo care. Conditions that usually subject a person to civil commitment include mental illness, developmental retardation, mental retardation, alcoholism, drug dependency, or some combination of these factors. Approximately 75% of the states have some statutory provision governing the involuntary commitment of drug-dependent persons

(Garcia & Keilitz, 1990). In these states, the laws limit involuntary civil commitments to drug-dependent persons in need of treatment and care, who are likely to be dangerous to themselves or others, or who are unable to meet their basic needs for sustenance, shelter, and self-protection. Pregnant drug users may be subject to laws that find them to be dangers to themselves because of their actions, or maternal addiction may be deemed to endanger an "other" with protectable rights. Addicts may lose their maternal rights as well as their rights to liberty in civil proceedings because they are considered dangerous, even though no criminal charge can be made.

When pregnant drug users are charged with any offense, they can be subject to the discretionary orders of the judge before whom they appear. For example, judges throughout the country are sentencing pregnant drug offenders to enter drug treatment facilities. Prosecutors are also arguing successfully that release from jail or prison be made conditional on completion of drug treatment. Judicial discretion also can affect the length of sentence imposed. Sometimes judges impose longer sentences on pregnant drug users. In 1993, 489 pregnant women were being held in state corrections institutions (in 47 states for which there were reports), and 105 pregnant inmates were in federal custody. During that year, there were 789 reported births to inmates (Maguire & Pastore, 1994). Many more went uncounted because inmates delivered in community facilities and then returned to the state or federal prison to complete their sentences. These are only a small proportion of the pregnant women being detained. The number of pregnant inmates serving terms in county jails and local facilities is not available. It is likely that most crack addicts are sentenced to misdemeanor terms in local corrections facilities to detain them until their babies are born.

Jailing pregnant drug users may not reduce harm to the fetus at all. In jail, where the mother may be experiencing extreme stress, there actually may be an increased chance of fetal distress. In addition, pregnant women may not get adequate medical care. Health care providers within the criminal justice system are neither well equipped nor prepared to handle obstetrics.

When judges tailor a woman's sentence to her reproductive status, the resulting harsher treatment has an impact not only for the individual being sentenced but for all women in general. Women who suffer from drug or alcohol dependency and AIDS do not exist in a social, political, and economic vacuum, yet when policy calls for criminalization and medicalization for these problems, each individual is treated without consideration of her environmental concerns. The conditions of poverty, discrimination, unemployment, inadequate health care services, and violence against women are not addressed. General social problems underlying the symptoms confronted in criminal courts and crisis health care treatment are ignored (Bagley & Merlo, 1995).

Women who do seek help for drug addiction during pregnancy cannot get it. Two-thirds of the hospitals surveyed by the House Select Committee reported they had no drug treatment programs to which their pregnant patients could be referred; none reported the availability of special programs geared to providing comprehensive drug treatment and prenatal care (Kasinsky, 1993). Without treatment, prosecutions are simply punitive stopgaps, and reporting laws force poor women of minority groups to surrender their children (Humphries, 1993).

Fetal Endangerment

Fundamental Rights. The use of narcotics and cocaine already is illegal. Many states have found it sufficient simply to enforce already existing laws rather than add penalties for pregnant women. When laws make actions criminal that only women can commit, the laws are, by their nature, discriminatory.

Prosecutions by the criminal justice system for drug use have been of predominantly poor women of minority backgrounds who have given birth to drug-exposed babies. Between 1987 and 1991, at least 165 women in 26 states were arrested on criminal charges because of their drug behavior during pregnancy. Tens of thousands more women have had their children removed from them and taken into custody by welfare agencies. Poor women have been prosecuted by a largely white social welfare establishment; more than half of all the recent prosecutions of pregnant women were of women of color (Kasinsky, 1993).

Women are being prosecuted for behavior that *may be* harmful without proof that the behavior *has been* harmful. The failed duty of these women is failure to avoid risk, not failure to avoid harm (Reed, 1993).

Rights of Women. There has been increasingly outspoken opposition of public health organizations to prosecutions of cocaine-addicted pregnant women (Paltrow, 1990). The very nature of the problem mandates that whatever action criminal justice authorities may take will be possible only with the cooperation and support of health care providers.

Health care providers are being asked to supply information to legal and criminal authorities if pregnant patients are using cocaine. It is not clear by what judicial standard a mother may have her acts of commission and omission while pregnant made subject to state scrutiny (Paltrow, 1990). Health care providers are being asked to take on a role outside the purview of their professions. As informants for the state, they are also acting in potential violation of patients' rights.

Rather than a focus on criminalization of pregnant addicts, a more comprehensive and complex policy is needed. Instead of filtering pregnant substance abusers through the costly process of criminalization, women in need of care can be identified by outreach workers in their neighborhoods. Some drug treatment programs have employed former addicts as outreach workers. Workers go to laundromats, grocery stores, and crack houses searching for pregnant women on drugs. These neighborhood workers are more likely than others to be effective in encouraging pregnant women to seek care and helping them find appropriate drug treatment, health care, and family services (Appel, 1992).

When compared with that of other industrialized countries, the infant mortality rate is high in the United States, and the rate of infant death has climbed since the 1970s. Despite a high standard of living, the United States ranks low on this significant indicator of quality of life. Improving the status of the nation in this important area will come only when all pregnant women are provided with quality prenatal care and assistance before and throughout their pregnancies. Making infant mortality a priority for change means addressing the multiple health care problems of all childbearing women (Merlo, 1993).

Structural Issues. To some, laws relating to family life are important because of their direct effect in coercing compliance. The real importance of these laws is that they set the outer limits of what the community regards as morally tolerable (Johnson, 1990). Prohibitory laws show that concern is not really focused on the well-being of infants, nor that of their mothers. Drastic action toward cocaine mothers and other substance abusers reflects public fear and loathing toward crack cocaine. The risks faced by pregnant women in the workplace and in substandard housing without adequate health care are not considered; instead, responsibility for the fetus is made a personal responsibility.

In assessing blame, criminal law focuses on the past. A wiser approach is to look toward the future, in which the well-being of both the mother and the child should be of equal importance to a society that has an interest in producing future generations of healthy people.

Case Study of a Crack Mom:
Jennifer Johnson

On July 13, 1989, Jennifer Johnson, age 23, was convicted in Sanford, Florida, of delivering cocaine to her newborn daughter through the umbilical cord. She also was charged with giving birth to a son in 1987 with traces of cocaine in his system. It was reported that all four of her children were cocaine-affected.

Johnson's case was the first success by a state in using drug trafficking charges to regulate behavior during pregnancy. Johnson was sentenced to 15 years of probation, including 1 year of strict supervision in a drug rehabilitation program with monthly random urine testing. She was required to achieve her high school equivalency degree and perform 200 hours of community service while remaining employed. She also was required to enter an intensive prenatal care program if she ever became pregnant again (Kasinsky, 1993). Under state law, Johnson could have received a 30-year prison term (Curriden, 1990).

Even though the convictions eventually were overturned, they had broad public support. A survey of 15 southern states by the *Atlanta Constitution* found that 71% of the 1,500 people polled favored criminal penalties for pregnant women whose illegal drug use injured their babies. More women than men were in favor of criminalizing "fetal abuse" (Curriden, 1990).

According to the prosecutor in Johnson's case, Jeff Deen, criminal charges were the only way to stop her from using cocaine. As he said, "We arrested her at a crack house. . . . She wasn't doing anything to help herself. The arrest is what motivated her to get help that she wasn't getting on her own."

Before the delivery of her daughter in January, 1989, Johnson had delivered three other cocaine-affected babies. All four of her children were in the custody of relatives. Deen believed that Johnson "had used up all her chances. We needed to make sure this woman does not give birth to another cocaine baby. The message is that this community cannot afford to have two or three cocaine babies from the same person."

Johnson was not grateful for the state intervention. She said, "I am a recovering addict. I cannot change the fact that I did it, and I'm sorry. There are many other women out there with cocaine babies. Why me?"

According to Assistant State Attorney Deen, he knew he could not prove fetal abuse. "We knew Florida law didn't cover actions to the fetus, so the prosecution had to focus on injuries sustained at the time of birth." Florida Circuit Judge O. H. Eaton, Jr., found Johnson guilty in a nonjury trial. He said that she could not use her addiction or her pregnancy as an excuse for illegal behavior. "The choice to use or not to use cocaine is just that . . . a choice," he said. "Once the defendant made that choice she assumed responsibility for the natural consequences of it. Children, like all persons, have the right to be free from having cocaine introduced into their systems by others" (Curriden, 1990).

According to newspaper reports in June, 1989, about Johnson's upcoming trial, she was an unwed mother of 23 when she gave birth for the second time to a baby with traces of cocaine in her system. She was quoted as saying she was sorry, but she did not believe that criminal prosecution would help her. She was living in a drug treatment center while her aunt and mother cared for her four children.

Deen was reported to contend that the prosecution was a way to hold mothers responsible for drug use. "She had this [drug] problem for many years, and she continued to have cocaine babies," Deen said. "That's one of the reasons we decided to prosecute this case" (Howard, 1989).

In July, 1989, immediately following the hearing, newspaper accounts quoted Judge Eaton's ruling that "A derivative of cocaine which the defendant had introduced into her body passed through the newborn's umbilical cord." The judge said, "I am convinced and find that a child who is born but whose umbilical cord has not been severed is a 'person' within the intent and meanings of Florida Statute 893.13. I am convinced and find that the 'delivery' includes the passage of cocaine or a derivative of it from the body of a mother into the body of her child through the umbilical cord after the birth occurs."

According to newspaper accounts, Jennifer Johnson sat impassively during the trial and as the verdict was read. She refused to comment. Her defense attorney, Jim Sweeting, said he would appeal. He believed that the ruling would be a signal to pregnant addicts to avoid prenatal care and to give birth to their babies outside hospitals.

The judge noted the argument but disagreed: "I believe the opposite to be true . . . that pregnant addicts are placed on notice that they have a responsibility to seek treatment" (*Daytona Beach News Journal*, July 14, 1989, p. 3A).

The Florida state appeals court ruled in 1991 to uphold Johnson's convictions. Newspaper accounts at the time explained that the court had found that Jennifer Johnson had acted essentially as a drug pusher.

The ruling was divided (2-1) and headed for the Florida Supreme Court. The appeals judges said that the matter was of "great importance and the state's highest court needs to decide once and for all."

Appeals Court Judge James Kauksch wrote that Johnson,

> voluntarily took cocaine into her body, knowing it would pass to her fetus and knowing (or should have known) that birth was imminent. She is deemed to know that an infant is a person, and a minor and that delivery of cocaine to the infant is illegal.

In the other consenting opinion, Judge Cobb agreed, saying "It is no undue burden upon an expectant mother to avoid cocaine use during the last several days of pregnancy."

Opposition from Judge Winifred Sharp was strongly worded. She said that the law in question did not apply to the birthing process. Lynn Paltrow, an American Civil Liberties Union lawyer who represented Johnson during the appeal, called the ruling a "slap in the Legislature's face." According to the press, the case was being watched closely in Florida and elsewhere.

Jennifer Johnson still declined comment. She was reported to have finished her 1-year court-ordered treatment and to be counseling other patients in drug rehab (Brazil & Salamone, 1991).

Finally, in July of 1992, the Florida State Supreme Court overturned the convictions. The press reported that the court had invalidated the prosecution strategy of using "delivery of a controlled substance to a minor" by a mother during the birthing process as a way of bringing a criminal conviction against a cocaine-addicted woman. According to Johnson's attorney, Paltrow, in her press report, "It's an enormous victory for public health, women, and newborns in Florida. The ruling makes it clear that Florida's policy is to treat pregnant women, not imprison them."

Jennifer Johnson cried when she was told of the decision. "Does this mean I'm not a criminal any more?" she reportedly asked her lawyer. At the time of the successful appeal, Johnson was in treatment in Largo, Florida. She had relapsed after the first appeal was denied in 1991 (Hatcher, 1992).

The following edited summary of the decision in the Johnson case comes from *The Southern Reporter*. All justices concurred with the decision written by Harding.

> The issue before the court is whether section 893.13(1)(c)(1), Florida Statutes (1989) permits the criminal prosecution of a mother, who ingested

a controlled substance prior to giving birth, for delivery of a controlled substance to the infant during the thirty to ninety seconds following the infant's birth, but before the umbilical cord is severed. Johnson presents four arguments attacking her conviction: 1) the interpretation of the statute violates the legislature's intent; 2) the plain language of the statute prevents her conviction; 3) the conviction violates her constitutional rights of due process and privacy; and 4) the state presented insufficient evidence to show that she intentionally delivered cocaine to a minor.

The record in this case establishes the following facts. On October 3, 1987, Johnson delivered a son. The birth was normal with no complications, no fetal distress. . . . Johnson admitted that she used cocaine the night before she delivered. A basic toxicology test performed on Johnson and her son was positive for benzoylecgonine, a metabolite or "breakdown" product of cocaine.

In December 1988, Johnson, while pregnant with a daughter, suffered a crack overdose. Johnson told paramedics that she had taken $200 of crack cocaine earlier that evening and that she was concerned about the effects of the drug on her unborn child. Johnson was then taken to the hospital for observation.

Johnson was hospitalized again on January 23, 1989 when she was in labor. Johnson told the obstetrician that she had used rock cocaine that morning while she was in labor. With the exception of finding meconium stain fluid in the amniotic sack, there were no other complications with the birth of Johnson's baby daughter. The following day, the Dept. of Health and Rehabilitative Services investigated an abuse report of a cocaine baby. Johnson told the investigator that she had smoked pot and crack cocaine three to four times every-other-day throughout the duration of her pregnancy. Johnson's mother acknowledged that Johnson had been using cocaine for at least three years during the time her daughter and son were born. (*Johnson v. State*, 1991)

In overturning her criminal conviction, Justice Harding wrote,

Before Johnson can be prosecuted under this statute, it must be clear that the Legislature intended for it to apply to the birthing process. . . . I can find no case where delivery of a drug was based on an involuntary act such as diffusion and blood flow.

At oral argument, the state acknowledged that no other jurisdiction has upheld a conviction of a mother for delivery of a controlled substance to an infant through either the umbilical cord or an in utero transmission; nor has the state submitted any subsequent authority to reflect that this fact has changed. The court declines that state's invitation to walk down a path that the law, public policy, reason and common sense forbid it to tread. Therefore we quash the decision, answer the question in the negative, and remand with directions that Johnson's other convictions be reversed.

It is so ordered. (*Johnson v. State*, 1991)

3. Treatment for Women Who Abuse Crack Cocaine

An important issue for women who abuse crack cocaine is the increasing need for treatment programs that consider gender-specific problems. The National Association of State Alcohol and Drug Abuse Directors (NASADAD) examined 1.2 million admissions to 7,743 alcohol and drug treatment units. It found that 22.3% of admissions for treatment of alcoholism were women and 33% of admissions to programs for treatment of other substance abuse were women. Younger patients admitted for treatment of alcoholism were more likely to be female than those in older age groups, suggesting that there is a continuing increase in female substance abuse (Center for Substance Abuse Treatment [CSAT], 1994).

Generally, when treatment is available for those who abuse drugs, the results are positive. Studies indicate that most abusers show a favorable response to the initiation of any treatment process. Outcomes are more favorable for patients who are able to be engaged in frequent, longer-term treatment programs (Khalsa, Paredes, & Anglin, 1993).

Although treatment for crack-abusing women has a positive outlook, too often patients do not complete treatment. Retention rates in short- and long-term treatment centers for drug abusers have been increasing in the past decade. Nevertheless, dropout still remains the rule in all treatment modalities and phases (DeLeon, 1993). A substance abuser may not complete treatment the first, second, or even the third time she enters. While she is in treatment, however, she is not as likely to be self-destructive or destructive to others, and with each successive attempt at positive change, there is benefit to the patient and to the community.

Crack Treatment:
Concepts and Issues

Programs offering treatment for crack abusers developed from models that originally had been used with alcoholics, heroin addicts, and intranasal cocaine users. Many of the processes of treatment are the same regardless of the substance involved. In addition, most crack users can be categorized as "polydrug" users; that is, they are likely to have a long history of substance abuse and to use other drugs as well as crack. Treatment for crack, therefore, cannot be considered separately from treatment for other substances, and patients must be viewed against a background of many factors.

Because the process is a complex one, treatment for drug addiction may be carried out in different forms or formats. At present, treatment facilities include detoxification, medical services, residential services, day treatment, self-help groups, family services, and case management. In the review that follows, the special issues of crack treatment are described within the context of substance abuse treatment in general.

Detoxification Services

Those who have gone through withdrawal from crack describe an experience of uncontrollable urges. The symptoms are mostly mental. Although drug withdrawal usually is thought to take about 28 days, the binge nature of crack use makes the withdrawal process more variable. A patient may experience extreme distress from time to time for many years as she relives the withdrawal process again and again.

Withdrawal is the first in a series of five neurobehavioral stages of recovery from drug addiction described by researchers. These stages were derived from the experiences of cocaine abusers as they progressed through the first months of their recovery. During the first stage, withdrawal, patients are disoriented, depressed, and fatigued and feel very much out of control. The honeymoon stage follows, during which cravings are reduced, mood improves, energy increases, and confidence and optimism return. During "the wall," patients face a major hurdle, with high relapse vulnerability because of low energy, difficulty concentrating, irritability, and insomnia. The adjustment stage involves a great feeling of accomplishment and accommodation to the lifestyle changes that began in previous stages, and a new definition of self emerges. Finally, during the resolution stage, there is a shift from learning new skills to monitoring for relapse signs. Reaching resolution signals that the patient has developed strong personal goals for maintaining a balanced lifestyle and involvement with other interests. Unfortunately, many addicts never reach resolution because their access to treatment is limited.

The series of five stages described above is the basis for a 6-month treatment program called the neurobehavioral approach. In this model, information, support, and encouragement are structured to address each of the five stages (Rawson, Obert, McCann, Smith, & Ling, 1993). Even after the 6 months of neurobehavioral treatment, extensive follow-up work is still needed for the patient who has abused drugs for years. Needless to say, treatment may be a lifelong process.

Detoxification usually is the first step of the treatment process and is designed to assist a patient during the withdrawal process. There may be any number of physical and emotional responses when the user stops smoking crack. Problems with sleeping and eating often accompany irrational thinking and poor judgment. Some of the responses may be due to the effects of drug withdrawal on the body. Other responses may be due to the lifestyle the user had been living before abruptly finding herself in detox. Users often report nightmares and feeling irritable and jumpy. Health problems are likely in the self-destructive lifestyle of Crackworld. Still other responses come from fear and desperation when the crack smoker finds herself in detox with no escape from this reality.

The aim of detoxification is to stabilize the heavy drug user until her body is relatively free of drugs. This process generally takes from 21 to 45 days, depending on how long the user had been continuously using crack (and/or other drugs) prior to her entry. Detox is best performed on an inpatient basis (Lyman & Potter, 1991).

Detox need not be voluntary. If a judge decides that the lifestyle of an individual shows threat of harm to herself or others, she can be forced to submit to a program of withdrawal. Whether patients voluntarily submit or are ordered by a court into a detox facility, there is a need for supervision and round-the-clock attention for all patients.

Substance abusers often report that they have gone through the detoxification process while in jail. Their arrests for drug-related or other charges may have been the incident that forced them to stop using. There are risks with using jails as detox facilities, especially for pregnant women. It is unlikely that jails are equipped or prepared to handle the emergencies that can arise as a patient's body goes through the drastic changes from withdrawal. It is also unlikely that jail inmates get the kind of crisis intervention that would assist them in making positive long-term changes. In many jails, for example, a "suicide watch" is a humiliating experience in which all garments and instruments that might be used to commit suicide are removed and the patient/inmate is kept in an open area for constant impersonal scrutiny by numerous strangers.

Medical Services

Pharmacological agents have been prescribed for substance abusers to assist with specific aspects of treatment. There are medications recommended for overdose, for example, that counteract the negative effects of a lethal dose of drugs. There are other medications that are recommended to help alleviate the pain and physical distress sometimes associated with withdrawal. Some treatment providers recommend medications meant to reduce the intense craving and offer relaxation to the patient. At other stages in the treatment process, medications may provide stabilization and balance for the patient. In still other cases, medication is needed for the treatment of comorbid conditions, psychiatric symptoms such as depression, anxiety, or schizophrenia (Schottenfeld, Carroll, & Rounsaville, 1993).

The development of medications to treat cocaine abuse has become a major research initiative of the National Institute on Drug Abuse (NIDA). The tricyclic antidepressant desipramine is the first medication to receive substantial support for its efficacy. Buprenorphine has shown utility in the treatment of cocaine abuse combined with opiate addiction. Other drugs presently being tested for their efficacy in treating cocaine abuse include lithium, methadone, bronocripine, amantadine, dopa, apomorphine, nimodipine, mazindol, sertraline, flupenthixol, calcium channel blockers, and antiseizure medications such as carbamazepine (Johnson & Vocci, 1993; Kosten, 1991).

Depression is a comorbid condition often found in substance abusers. It has been treated successfully with medications. In one study of the psychopathology of cocaine abusers, women constituted approximately 25% of patients admitted to a hospital for cocaine treatment. Major depression was diagnosed in 23.5% of women, compared with 4.2% of men. Females also were found to improve more slowly from depression than were male patients. In addition, antisocial personality disorder was discovered in 22% of the men, but there were no women diagnosed as aggressive (Weiss, Mirin, Griffin, & Michael, 1988).

One indicator that depression is an important medical issue in treatment for crack addiction is the high suicide rate associated with crack use. Studies have found that the percentage of crack abusers reporting at least one suicide attempt is higher than that those whose primary addiction was another drug, such as alcoholics or heroin addicts (DeLeon, 1993). In most cases, patients recover from depression in time, with or without treatment. With treatment, however, much of the destructive and self-destructive behavior associated with depression can be minimized.

When medical services are part of the treatment program, there are some ethical issues that cannot be avoided. Compelled medical treatment, which would not be considered for others who use crack, is sometimes authorized when the patient is pregnant. Many individuals, as well as medical doctors, would agree to exceptional treatment of pregnant women, but according to the *Journal of the American Medical Association*, neither the medical profession nor society should support compelled medical treatment of pregnant women. If members of society and health care providers are truly interested in enhancing fetal health, their efforts should be directed toward increasing the availability and quality of voluntary prenatal care for all pregnant women. Drug and alcohol rehabilitation programs and other social services should also be made available for those pregnant women who need them (O'Sullivan & Dooley, 1990).

The overwhelming reason why most health professionals oppose involuntary testing and treatment is that many women, fearful of punishment, will avoid the health care system altogether. The health of those with high-risk pregnancies, who are most in need of prenatal care, would be most in jeopardy.

Physicians have an ethical obligation to be advocates for the fetus when a pregnant woman is making choices. This advocacy may include the use of persuasion or influence but not the use of threats, lies, or physical force (Nelson & Milliken, 1988).

Residential Treatment

Substance abuse treatment can be more intense and complete if the patient resides in the program. Outside influences can be minimized, and residents are kept involved in the process full-time. Entering, and staying in, a residential treatment program implies that the patient can put the rest of her life "on hold" while she receives treatment. In some cases, she has no choice, and a higher authority may order placement in some type of residential program or incarceration. As long as the patient is away from family and community, however, the treatment process and her ability to function in a normal setting remain untested.

Many pregnant crack users find themselves sentenced to state and federal prison for their drug use or for other charges. It may seem to those who recommend these sentences that imprisonment is one way to make sure that the mother remains drug-free until the baby is born. Prisons, however, are not drug-free environments. Although the mother may not smoke crack while in prison, there is no way to force her to take care of her health if she has chosen to be self-destructive.

Imprisonment can be very stressful for pregnant inmates and those who have recently given birth. Pregnant inmates have physical disadvantages that make it more difficult to cope with the demands of incarceration. There may be psychological stress over whether to have an abortion, what should be done with the child after birth, and how to cope with separation from other children.

Newborn children of incarcerated mothers may face long-term problems of their own. An infant who does not have a continuous, intimate relationship with his or her mother during the first 2 years after birth is more likely to develop one or more of the following traits: psychopathology, inability to relate to others, difficulty with intimacy and assertiveness, lack of trust in others, lack of willpower, indecisiveness, fear of abandonment, fear of new experiences, and poor academic performance (Woolredge & Masters, 1993). Later on, children whose parents are incarcerated have a higher rate of teen pregnancy. Evidence is also accumulating that many of these children will follow in their parents' footsteps and will be incarcerated (Moses, 1995). Policies for the care and support of pregnant inmates in state correction facilities are in the process of improving and expanding, but they have a long way to go before they satisfy the needs of pregnant inmates or their children.

Day Treatment Services

Although residential treatment programs take away personal responsibility, day treatment programs offer more opportunities for relapse and have higher dropout rates. For example, one study that examined inpatient and day treatment programs for black male cocaine abusers found this population more likely to drop out of day treatment programs than inpatient programs. The study also found that it is less likely that these crack addicts will complete day treatment programs. Those who do complete day treatment programs were slightly less likely to relapse than were those who completed inpatient programs (Alterman, O'Brien, & Droba, 1993). This study and others indicate that day treatment may have the most enduring results if patients are actively involved and able to complete the program.

Had females been included in the research, they would be even more likely to be successful in avoiding relapse following completion of a day treatment program. Because most female addicts are mothers, there is extra incentive for recovery in this type of program. They may be able to keep their families together if they do not have to enter a residential program in order to get treatment. This likelihood has been noted in therapeutic community programs. As a response to the need for day treatment, some outpatient models for crack-addicted mothers have affiliated with community-based centers or urban hospitals (DeLeon, 1993).

Because most mothers who must participate in drug treatment can do so only on an outpatient basis, the design of the programs must take their special needs into account in order to be successful. Those special needs include structure—clear boundaries and well-defined rules and consequences; intensity—real involvement and meaningful support services; and frequency—numerous types of useful activities that absorb the patient's attention for most of her time. Structure, intensity, and frequency are the keys to making outpatient treatment effective.

Day treatment often is based on an agenda encompassing the following three stages. Stage 1 involves breaking the addictive cycle, establishing initial abstinence, assessing the severity of the patient's problem, and enhancing her motivation to change. Patients may attend four group sessions or more and at least one individual session per week. Stage 2 shifts the focus toward solidifying abstinence and learning specific relapse prevention skills. Patients may attend two group sessions and one individual session per week. Stage 3 consists of enrollment in a continuing care group that provides peer support and focuses on developing a long-range recovery plan or a psychotherapy group that addresses topics such as relationships, self-esteem, or sexuality.

Throughout the entire program, all patients may be urine tested on an unanticipated schedule. It may be necessary to test as frequently as twice per week, but all patients must be tested from time to time. Patients also are encouraged to develop a routine of attending self-help meetings (Washton, 1988).

The treatment process must have other elements in addition to counseling sessions. When psychotherapy has been used as the sole treatment for cocaine abusers, the results have been limited. Psychotherapy also can be used with pharmacotherapy, but in these cases, it is usually found that psychotherapy is secondary and supportive to the use of medications, rather than the use of pharmacotherapy being a support for psychotherapeutic counseling (Carroll, 1992). Patients need practice with new behaviors and training in living stable lives. Treatment that is "all talk" is not as likely to result in long-term, positive change as that which provides for behavior change as well as attitude change.

Self-Help Groups

Self-help groups are essential to day treatment programs as well as residential treatment. Self-help programs have been used for primary cocaine addiction and for cocaine addiction combined with other addictions. They are appropriate while the patient is actively participating in a treatment program and afterward. Self-help groups also can provide a practical continuing care service for long-term, stabilized patients.

Historically, the most popular and widely used self-help model is that of 12-step recovery programs including Alcoholics Anonymous (AA), Narcotics Anonymous (NA), and Cocaine Anonymous (CA). There are many important benefits of 12-step programs, one of them being their ongoing nature. A member can go to a meeting at any place or time and know what to expect. Substance abusers know that they will receive encouragement and understanding at an NA meeting. Meetings are widely available, and there are no fees.

Self-help groups serve as a valuable source for social support, peer identification, and role modeling. The 12-step philosophy offers useful concepts for relapse prevention and successful recovery. Members gain strength and security along with practical strategies for surviving "one day at a time." According to the view of 12-step programs, recovery is a lifelong process involving permanent changes in attitude and lifestyle (Kleber, 1994).

Family Services

Treatment for cocaine-abusing women must serve the patient in the context of familiar relationships. Most of them have children, and few of them have responsible male partners to provide for them. If responsibility and autonomy are the goals for rehabilitation of cocaine-abusing mothers, then they must be considered in their environment, not separate from their life situations.

In some cases, treatment must involve separation from the addict's immediate environment in order to break the habits and daily patterns that are part of her substance abuse. It may be necessary to isolate the patient for a while to allow for detoxification, orientation, and diagnosis. Separating mothers from children and addicts from families is a costly side effect of this aspect of treatment.

To overcome detrimental effects of separation, other aspects of treatment must consider the social, emotional, and familiar environment of the abuser and how she can live within that environment without drug abuse. Children and other family members must be considered. Facilities and resources for family participation in treatment must be included as basic to the process. For example, if a program does not provide child care, neither inpatient nor day treatment is truly available to women with children, who are the majority of substance-abusing women (CSAT, 1994). Uniting women and their children in treatment is called the reunification model (CSAT, 1994).

The possibility of having their children reunited with them is often an incentive for mothers to enter treatment. Under supervision, mothers can learn parenting skills and experience improved relationships with their children. Intervention during a time of stress can lead in a positive direction for all the patients' family relationships. Keeping mothers and children together during treatment unburdens foster care systems by ensuring the safety of children in a therapeutic milieu.

Case Management Services

Case management is a critical component of any substance abuse treatment program. It is essential for programs that provide comprehensive treatment to have a case manager who has access to and can coordinate the numerous sources of services. Treatment services usually involve multiple disciplines and many different care providers. A case manager brings all the services, agencies, and resources together in a comprehensive framework. Case management involves developing a personalized plan of action directed toward treatment goals. Treatment plans take the particular needs of the patient into account, but they must necessarily also consider availability of services (CSAT, 1994).

Analysis of the
Phases of Development

The Development of Treatment Programs

To analyze the development of treatment services for crack mothers, it is useful to have an analytical tool that can be used in any treatment context and by various kinds of analysts. Such a heuristic device makes it possible to view the evolution of treatment for crack mothers through a series of phases as it fits into other dimensions of social life. In addition to being useful for studying results, this analytical tool also can be helpful in the planning process. Such an analytical tool is applicable to specific cases as well as to general developments.

Considering treatment services with a heuristic tool or any such imposed pattern is useful only if it allows one also to see those issues that are special and most important for a particular group such as crack mothers. Looking at the overall context sometimes makes it unlikely that specifics will come to light. Meaningful analysis comes only from taking the particulars into consideration as well as the general patterns.

Dividing the process into phases provides alternatives for focus. Within each phase, there are different emphases that must be considered essential for successful treatment by planners and treatment providers. Each of the phases also includes the elements of conflict that can lead to the demise of the program as well as lack of success for patients.

Concepts for the four analytical phases of treatment come from the ideas of Richard Quinney and his study of the social reality of crime (1970). Although his focus is on the economics of crime, his work proves useful in an analysis of the treatment process. Quinney's view focuses on the context as it is reflected in the individual, rather than simply the individual as a reflection of the context. This social perspective is significant because it is important to remember that the treatment process implies broad societal changes, not merely changes in the attitudes of a crack mother.

Phases of Development

As it developed, treatment for crack mothers went through four phases that were predictable and found in other social service programs.

Patients also pass through the same phases as they progress in recovery. The phases of development correspond with the four neurobiological stages of withdrawal, honeymoon, the wall, and adjustment for the patient. The four phases are: definition and development of the problem, implementation of programs, routinization of services, and review and redo.

Phase 1: Definition and development. In 1986, crack addiction became recognized as a social problem in response to media attention. From the beginning, the problem of pregnant crack users was surrounded by controversy. The most controversial issues related to conflicts between responsibility for the welfare of children and the need to provide for personal autonomy. This is a social conflict that appears to be a personal problem. Crack mothers are held responsible for their children, but no one is being held responsible for the decaying neighborhoods that prove most hazardous for the welfare of those children.

The real issues at stake have been lost in the controversy about the legal rights of children. Because there are conflicting values involving the question of family autonomy in United States society, a difference of public opinion about crack-abusing mothers was inevitable. It is with cases involving crack mothers that we have begun the difficult process of weighing family rights against the rights of children to live decent lives (Besharov, 1990a, 1990b). State intervention in family matters has not provided real improvement in the lives of the children who are at stake.

In the continuum of the state's response to prenatal substance abuse, from public health to prosecution, child welfare falls in the middle. This position places the welfare of children in the middle of the debate swirling around criminalizing prenatal conduct. Often, the important common ground is overlooked. Advocates of both public health and prosecution favor treatment and prevention. They disagree on the means, not the ends (Horowitz, 1990).

What is best for children usually is not found in the midst of controversy. Even though they may be removed from their mother's custody, many children of crack-addicted parents are not readily adopted. For them, terminating parental rights is cutting the last tie to their biological families. Even though some parents will conquer their drug problems in time, their children are lost to a series of foster homes or other state facilities.

The issue of race is significant, because crack takes its greatest toll on those least able to bear the burden. In California in 1990, for the first time in that state's history, the absolute number of black children in foster care exceeded the number of whites, even though less than 10% of the state's children were black. A policy that translates into taking children away from their parents and falls most heavily on minority communities should make everyone think twice (Besharov, 1990b).

Part of the controversy surrounding crack cocaine was fed by an image of a violent subculture of users. With time, as the image has sharpened, it has grown even more violent. Many women in treatment for drug addiction have been exposed to violence in the past, and many may be vulnerable to continued violence in their communities and in their own personal relationships. The family unification model is a sensitive issue when it is used in treatment with a family in which abuse is likely to continue (CSAT, 1994).

It may be that mothers must learn alternatives to violence as ways to control their children. It may be that fathers must learn alternatives to violence to establish relationships in their families. In some cases, there are sound treatment methods for changing violent family patterns, but for the child who lives in a violent neighborhood where there is an active crack market, violence is part of the lifestyle. Children growing up in these environments need special treatment for the trauma they are likely to feel. Any real treatment also must address neighborhood issues and the crack market characteristics that are the real problem for the children.

Phase 2: Implementation. In 1989, community agencies began innovative programs to address concerns related to crack-addicted mothers and their children. After 1990, nearly every city and large community had opened at least one program for treatment of crack mothers. Successful programs for crack-addicted women were built on the models for treatment that had been effective with other substance abuse problems. There was no lack of models for treatment or ideas for programs, yet despite the solid historical foundation, only a few initial programs have remained open.

Treatment was available to only a few of those who needed it in 1990. Despite increased need, resources for treatment began declining after 1994. According to those concerned with treatment for women at the U.S. Center for Substance Abuse Treatment, Division of Clinical Programs, Women and Children's Branch (CSAT, 1994), the lack of access to treatment for women is serious. There are too few programs that offer appropriate and high-quality services that address the needs of women and children. They found that cost-effective, gender-specific treatment and recovery services for women simply were not available to those who need them.

Gender-specific counseling addresses low self-esteem; race and ethnicity issues; pregnancy issues; family relationships; attachment to unhealthy interpersonal relationships; interpersonal violence, including incest, rape, and other abuse; eating disorders; sexuality; parenting issues; grief and loss in life and in the family; appearances; creating a support system; developing a life plan; and recreational and leisure time activities for women and families (CSAT, 1994). Only some of these counseling themes are really gender-specific. Cost-effective programs integrate gender-specific treatment for women into programs that also offer related services for men.

For treatment to be successful, the patient must make permanent changes in habitual behaviors and responses. In the implementation or honeymoon phase of treatment, intervention may have more lasting influence if it is used to bring about multiple changes in behavior rather than simply to stop the use of crack.

The goals for each patient should be outlined in a comprehensive treatment plan during Phase 1. The likelihood of success in Phase 2 is highly dependent on the extent to which major changes in the patient's lifestyle, which were drawn up in that treatment plan, actually are achieved. Her reliance on drug reinforcement must be suppressed. She must learn alternative sources of reinforcement that provide satisfaction and are not self-destructive. The patient must increase her prosocial behaviors and decrease her antisocial or self-destructive behaviors (Grabowski, Higgins, & Kirby, 1993). She must learn to respond to different sources of pleasure and find other ways to achieve personal gratification. These are no small lessons.

Two problem areas that are important for crack-abusing women and must be considered during Phase 2 when treatment is implemented are sexuality and depression. The association between compulsive sexual behaviors and compulsive use of cocaine needs to be better understood in order to strengthen relapse prevention efforts (Tims & Leukefeld, 1993). The following three types of strategies are useful in addressing sexuality issues: educational workshops about sex and drugs, group counseling about sexual problems and sexuality, and medical and psychological assessment for sexually dysfunctional patients who may be the victims of sexual abuse or rape (CSAT, 1994).

Treatment programs also must include an ongoing HIV/AIDS education, prevention, and treatment component. Legal assistance should be provided for women with AIDS who may need help drawing up a will or establishing care and custody for their children. In addition, women who test positive for HIV or have AIDS must have access to medical care, psychotherapy, and other types of support to address the issues of health and well-being (CSAT, 1994).

A second element that must be of concern in treatment for crack mothers is the likelihood of serious depression. Symptoms that often can alert treatment providers that a patient is suffering from depression are those related to eating and sleeping disorders. The primary feature indicating major depression is a sad, blue, depressed mood that is pervasive, occurring most of the day, every day for at least one month. Loss of interest or pleasure in almost all activities also is common. At least three or four of the following features should be present for a diagnosis of major depression: sleeping disorders, eating disorders, persistent low energy, feelings of worthlessness, speeding up or slowing down, difficulty with concentration, and hopeless thoughts or thoughts of suicide. If left untreated, major depression eventually may resolve itself spontaneously; however, it often significantly impairs ability to function, and there is a substantial risk for suicide (Kleber, 1994).

Treatment providers for crack mothers must take the possibility of suicide seriously. Plans must be in place that consider both the safety and the emotional health of the threatening patient. Children of potentially suicidal mothers also need special care.

Phase 3: Routinization. Early in the 1990s, treatment programs developed procedures and modified original objectives to meet the pragmatic demands of day-to-day operations. After some years of providing care for crack smokers, treatment outcomes were not as positive as some analysts would have liked. Cocaine abusers had been found to have a significantly higher likelihood of relapse after treatment than did other chemically dependent persons (O'Keefe, 1989). The likelihood of relapse is the critical element of the third phase of development.

One of the factors that has been noted to be important to relapse is the way crack is administered. Cocaine smokers have an even higher relapse tendency than intranasal users. There is a limit to the amount of cocaine that can be put in the nose, and the resulting high is less intense than when the drug is smoked. Smoking cocaine is the method that allows the user to ingest the greatest amount and experience the most drastic effects. For both physiological and psychological reasons, a crack smoker may return to use again and again.

There are other important considerations in relapse. For example, using other drugs, especially alcohol, may impair the crack smoker's judgment and be related to relapse. Drinking alcohol is also a social behavior that may lead a crack smoker into the company of others who smoke crack and encourage it.

A history of failure and having nothing to lose or look forward to also are factors related to relapse. In addition, a strong personal resolve to remain abstinent is important to avoiding relapse. Social support from others who avoid crack also provides a foundation for abstinence, along with valued relationships and a sense of well-being (Havassy, Wasserman, & Hall, 1993).

Relapse is difficult to define with crack users because of the tendency of users to binge rather than use continuously. A lapse into cocaine use may precede long periods of abstinence. Relapse actually is part of the learning process in recovery. In attempting to define relapse, treatment providers must consider a specified period of abstinence prior to the lapse as well as the return to a given level of use for a certain amount of time. For example, to determine if a patient is making progress, it is necessary to find out if periods of abstinence are getting longer and periods of relapse are getting shorter, as well as to take into consideration the amount and intensity of use.

Addicts in treatment find that they have environmental cues that have been associated with drug use in the past and can evoke physiological craving or withdrawal symptoms. When drug treatment is located in the community where crack is sold and the patient has used it, she may face many external cues that trigger sensations of craving or desperation. Extinction of the links between environmental cues and cocaine may be necessary to avoid relapse (O'Brien, Ehrman, & Ternes, 1993). This may mean that a change of environment is needed if treatment is to be successful, or the patient must learn to view the environment from a different perspective.

Education is a key element in preventing relapse. Patients must be taught to understand the cues by which they are affected. They must learn the multiple factors that drive their use. They must also learn that alcohol and marijuana often lead to a return to using crack, and that there is therefore a need for abstinence from all addictive substances (Washton, 1988).

An important consideration for treatment of crack mothers is that their abuse of crack often has impaired relationships with their children. Even if a mother is motivated to care for her child, it may be psychologically and realistically difficult for her to do so. Feelings of guilt and shame for being an "unfit mother" may lead to relapse and other self-destructive behavior. All phases of the treatment program and all staff must provide positive motivation and support for mothering. Patients must be given access to the social support systems that promote and sustain their roles as mothers (CSAT, 1994).

Pregnant patients who continue to use drugs, including alcohol, while in treatment pose special difficulties. Procedures such as providing warnings, extra counseling, urine screens, loss of privileges, and intensive supervision can be used. It is essential to retain pregnant patients in treatment, where they may benefit from supportive and medical services. Discharge exposes them to potential relapse and life on the street (Kleber, 1994).

Treatment providers also will be confronted by difficult situations regarding patients who are pregnant or mothers and these women's relationships with child protective services agencies. Program staff needs to be aware of state reporting requirements. Legal advice also must be available to patients concerning circumstances in which their right to confidentiality may be suspended. Reporting laws on maternal substance abuse and fetal exposure have a major impact on patients. A report on a substance-abusing mother could lead to the removal of her children. Alcohol and other drug use alone, however, usually is not the sole criterion for court intervention (Kleber, 1994). Strategies that involve punishment of pregnant addicts do not maximize the chances of healthy births and are of questionable legality (Jessup & Roth, 1988).

Phase 4: Review and redo. After 1995, evaluations began to lead to a redefinition of the problem and redevelopment of programs for assisting crack-addicted pregnant women. After nearly a decade, treatment providers have had some positive impact. Studies of treatment programs demonstrate that cocaine-dependent patients can show favorable outcomes and that treatment programs can be effective. An example of such success is the PAR Village, an experimental program for cocaine-abusing mothers with children in St. Petersburg, Florida. In a 3-year follow-up study of clients who received day treatment in this program, as well as those with long-term residential treatment, positive results were displayed with regard to employment, criminality, education, family relationships, and stability of lifestyle (Coletti, Kim, Newel, & MacDonald, 1995).

Time abstinent from cocaine is the one measure of success that has been observed in most of those who participate in treatment. The increase in time abstinent is significantly greater for those whose treatment consisted of either inpatient plus high-intensity day treatment or self-help, or high-intensity day treatment plus self-help. Clearly, client motivation to enter and become engaged in intensive, longer-term treatment is an important issue for further study (Khalsa et al., 1993).

From a more comprehensive view, time abstinent from cocaine may not be as significant as other goals in the process of recovery. In evaluations of treatment programs, even the most long-term assessments do not usually consider neighborhood and community factors, yet these are the very influences that are most important to the lifestyle changes necessary for recovery. For example, in the PAR Village evaluation, a drug abuser was considered to be successfully recovering if she was employed, not facing criminal charges, improving her educational level, maintaining family relationships, and carrying on a stable lifestyle. Each of these standards for evaluation is social, not personal. Success in these measures involves effective interaction with the system of employment, the justice system, the educational system, the family system, and the community support system. Although treatment is viewed through the social systems in which a client lives, her success is measured by personal performance.

When treatment for cocaine-abusing mothers is the goal, there must be changes in the neighborhood and community that can be measured in real opportunities. In these terms, treatment must consist of economic changes that improve the employment market, legal changes that provide justice without racist and class biases, meaningful education that addresses human diversity, resources to provide for the health and well-being of families, and productive leisure time activities that are available to everyone. Real treatment implies a redefinition of the problem.

Into the Future

Moving ahead means resolving or redirecting conflicts. Conflicts arising at each phase of development are part of the pattern. Examples from the development of treatment for crack mothers are useful for analysis and planning.

In the phase of definition, controversies about mothers' rights versus the rights of babies often distorted the real issues of health and well-being for both. In the phase of implementation, programs often omitted essential issues such as sexuality and depression. Agencies decided that the costs of treatment for pregnant addicts were simply too high. In the phase of routinization, the problem of relapse posed a significant obstacle. Treating the same patient again and again, relapse after relapse, seemed hopeless to those who did not understand the lifelong pattern of treatment. During the phase of review, a change is called for. It is important to expand the treatment process to include neighborhood and community treatment plans and goals for addressing the problems there, as well as the problems of individuals.

There have been significant decreases in cocaine use from its peak in 1985. Although use of crack cocaine has declined in recent years, cocaine was the substance most frequently mentioned in drug-related deaths in 1991. In addition, the number of cocaine-related emergency room treatments increased in 1991 (National Institute on Drug Abuse [NIDA], 1991). Other surveys suggest that the number of chronic, hard-core drug users has remained relatively unchanged since 1988. In addition, upsurges in illicit drug use among adolescents have threatened the previous progress made against casual drug use (Office of National Drug Control Policy, 1995). These observations point to a continuing need for treatment despite downward trends in cocaine use.

According to CSAT (1994),

> The general consensus among those foremost in the field of addiction is that, for most individuals, treatment and recovery services work best in the context of a community-centered, coordinated system of comprehensive services designed to assure a continuum of support for recovery.

As this analysis of the phases of treatment has shown, there are two key themes in treatment for crack-abusing women. Treatment programs must provide a comprehensive web of services within the community and linkages to community-based organizations for referrals and resources outside the program.

Among the services that will be provided within treatment programs, there are likely to be three significant developments for crack-dependent women (Tims & Leukefeld, 1993).

1. Identifying and systematically testing pharmacological agents that may be useful in achieving abstinence from cocaine and reducing the likelihood of relapse. NIDA has focused a great deal of attention on this fascinating area of treatment. Methadone programs are examples of treatments using one pharmacological agent as a substitute for another drug considered to be more dangerous. In some respects, the dangerousness of particular pharmacological agents may be linked to their illegality, as with heroin or cocaine. Substituting dependency on a legally prescribed psychoactive substance is beneficial to the cocaine or heroin addict only if the substituted drug—for example, methadone—has fewer side effects and causes less physical damage to the

patient. That is not always the result. Sometimes addicts to prescribed medications suffer more side effects and greater physical disability than they did when they were dependent on an illegal substance. If addicts cannot legally get the kinds of drugs that bring them the effects they seek, then a black market will provide them. In considering regulated use of other pharmacological agents in place of cocaine, various aspects of the issue must be taken into account. Decisions must be based on the positive advantages of a drug rather than its legality.

2. Understanding the outcomes of existing treatment programs using field studies and long-term outcome measures. There are treatment programs for crack-addicted mothers that have been operating for more than 5 years. More long-term measures of treatment considering the constellation of factors involved are now under way. Whether measures are based on field studies or statistical analysis, the tendency has been to focus on the changes in the individual rather than changes in her context—her employment opportunities, the educational system, the legal system, her family life, and her community environment.

There are two patterns important to personal treatment outcomes. First, a significant number of women involved in Crackworld have suffered life-long victimization. Treatment efforts must be focused on preventing child abuse and teaching parenting skills. Second, Crackworld develops in abandoned structures, in deteriorating neighborhoods, and in communities without hope. Treatment efforts include a focus on economics and community development.

3. Testing the efficacy of specific psychosocial interventions such as psychotherapies, behavioral treatments, and relapse prevention strategies. In addition to the various treatment strategies that have been mentioned in this review, there are other systems thought of as "alternative." Many of them deserve continued study and practice. Some examples follow, but they by no means constitute an exhaustive list. Many other "methods" are in use, and success in treatment is claimed by many different kinds of programs.

Yoga has been successful in treatment for substance abuse and other kinds of addictions for a long time. Acupuncture and acupressure are used to relax and refocus addicts. Hypnosis also has been used in successful treatment of many kinds of addictions. Various herbal and other natural health treatments also are reputedly helpful in substance abuse treatment. Natural remedies are said to restore balance and reduce cravings. Amino acids reportedly replenish the supply of neurotransmitters depleted by crack abuse. Physical exercises of many kinds also have been recommended for addiction treatment, including tai chi, dance, and running. There also are programs of philosophy such as transcendental meditation and programs for spiritual growth and development beyond addiction (Kleber, 1994). No one program can possibly meet all the needs for services that a cocaine-abusing woman is likely to have. All these alternative methods are clearly only part of the vast array of programs that must be in place if treatment goals are taken seriously.

In its study of treatment programs for women, CSAT (1994) considered ethical questions that inevitably arise when behavior change is imposed in the name of treatment. There are four ethical principles for treatment: autonomy—providing for the autonomy of the person is a goal of treatment; beneficence— treatment has beneficial goals for the person and for society in general; equity—each person is treated equally; and nonmalevolence—the program should do no harm (CSAT, 1994). In a paraphrasing of John Stuart Mill, it can be said that "Humans are greater gainers by suffering each other to live as seems good to themselves, than by compelling each to live as seems good to the rest."

Case Study of a Treatment Program: Hope House

Using the heuristic device introduced above, a case study of an actual treatment program was developed. The analysis was divided into the four phases of definition, implementation, routinization, and review and redo.

During the development of the program, the conflicts mentioned above were basic. Phase 1 was characterized by a hasty, if well-meaning, response to media controversy about crack babies in the community. Phase 2 was a period of putting the program into place, but essential issues necessary for gender-specific treatment were left out. Phase 3 turned out to be a time of relapse for the residents and obstacles for the directors and others responsible for the program. During Phase 4, adaptations and modifications made it possible for the program to survive and continue for more than five years.

The case study was based on observations and interviews. The researcher visited the program on a weekly basis from 1989 to 1995. As a volunteer instructor for residents as well as a consultant and adviser to the directors of the program, the researcher acted as a participant-observer.

Phase 1: Definition and Development

A program to address the problems of cocaine mothers in Volusia County, Florida, was developed in September, 1989, by a group of citizens living near one of the lowest-income areas in the city of Daytona Beach. It was meant to be a safe house for cocaine mothers and their children, located in one of the most crime-ridden neighborhoods in the city, the Pine Haven housing projects. It was called Hope House.

Furnishings and supplies were donated. The center was operated with the support of a black women's sorority. It was the dream of one of its leading members, a community activist who had worked as a social worker in the neighborhood for many years. During the first phase, there was no telephone in the house, nor was there a staff member present on a regular basis.

Pine Haven is the oldest, toughest federal housing project in the city. A newspaper series about the community in 1989 described sordid living conditions, open drug dealing, and a generally criminogenic environment (Howard, 1989). Despite the poverty and disorganization common to such projects, it was the site of a new and innovative approach to treatment. The community responded to the local controversy about cocaine babies by creating a haven in the heart of the crack market.

Hope House was a community response to the media attention brought by the problem of crack to the Pine Haven neighborhood. It opened after the local department of health and the state department of rehabilitative services had studied the problem and found numerous cases of babies born to crack-abusing women in Daytona Beach hospitals. All reports about crack babies indicated fear of escalating medical and other social costs.

Phase 2: Implementation

The city housing authority provided a five-bedroom unit in the Pine Haven project, rent-free. There was a large kitchen but only one bathroom. The apartment was not air conditioned, despite the Florida climate, nor were units kept warm during winter storms. Furnishings were bare essentials, and supplies were not always available. In short, the lifestyle provided was clean and secure and not much more.

Based on the cooperative efforts of the Volusia County Health Department, the State Department of Health and Rehabilitative Services, Daytona Beach Community College employment and training

programs, the Mary McCleod Bethune Community Center, and local
volunteers, services were to be provided for five women of childbearing
age with cocaine problems. Without full-time staff or case management, many of the residents' needs went unmet. The two important
issues of violence and victimization went largely unaddressed, and
sexuality was not a formal subject of counseling.

Hope House offered a minimum of 90 days of shelter. Most residents
were expected to stay longer. Crack-addicted women were admitted in
their seventh month of pregnancy. Before their seventh month, pregnant women depended on outpatient programs.

Eligibility requirements included a history of substance abuse involving cocaine or IV drug abuse, age of 18 years or older, some form of
prior drug rehabilitation or treatment, commitment to recovery, medical clearance, and freedom from suicidal or violent histories and/or
chronic mental illness.

Phase 3: Routinization

Of the first five women who were residents in Hope House, four
were pregnant when they arrived. Three of the four original residents
delivered babies during their stay in the program.

One of the babies born to a resident had extreme health problems.
She tested positive for the HIV virus. Her mother was 29 years old,
and this was her fifth delivery. All of her children had been taken from
her custody. According to her, she had not used drugs while pregnant
with any of her other four babies, but she said she had used drugs and
had other addictions since she was 14. Her use of crack had only begun
in the last year.

When this woman discovered she was pregnant, she denied it at first
and went on smoking to forget. Later, she continued to smoke crack
because someone told her it would cause a miscarriage. She stopped
smoking when she was about 4 months pregnant. It was harder for her
to face her baby's exposure to HIV than her own condition, having the
AIDS virus.

The second infant born to a resident of Hope House involved a
complicated and difficult labor, but the mother and baby appeared well
in the months following the delivery. The mother of this infant was 19
years old, and this was her second crack baby. Although her first baby
was born apparently unaffected, she already had lost custody of that
child. This mother believed that if she stopped smoking crack 30 days
before the baby was born, all the cocaine would have left her system by

the time she delivered. She had used crack extensively for more than 3 years but entered treatment and tried to quit because she was pregnant.

The third baby born to a resident of Hope House had no apparent problems, and both mother and baby were progressing well after delivery. In this case, the mother was 29 years old, and this was her seventh child. She lost custody of all the children. Some of them are in foster homes; the others have been cared for by relatives. According to her, her goal was to get her own home where she could take care of all of her children and build a life for herself and them.

The fourth resident left before delivering her baby and disappeared into street life. No official report of the outcome was made.

The fifth resident was not a cocaine mother. She had a history of drug abuse and treatment, and her role was described as "peer counselor." She was designated to be in charge in the absence of staff members. This resident-in-charge was the subject of many complaints from the other residents. She was implicated when crack use in Hope House was documented.

After the first 90 days of operation, Hope House was closed. All the residents were forced to leave. During the early months of 1990, disorganization and conflict hounded the organizers of Hope House because of the bad publicity it received in a local TV news report. In a series of television news shows about the local crack market, a Daytona Beach television reporter recorded attempted crack deals going on through the windows of Hope House. Residents openly admitted smoking crack in the house to the television audience. Crack use was reported by neighbors and other observers as well.

The local TV reporter concluded that the Pine Haven neighborhood, with its high rate of crack cocaine arrests and sales, was not a good place for a home for cocaine mothers. She observed, "If you were going to put someone on a diet, you wouldn't close them up in a chocolate factory would you?"

Phase 4: Review and Redo

The first, failed attempt to develop a community care facility for cocaine mothers in Daytona Beach provided important lessons that contributed to the long-term success of the program. In March, 1990, Hope House was reorganized, expanded, and reopened. It was larger, and the walls had been painted, but it was located in the same bleak environment. Hope House had become a part of an agency for drug rehabilitative services called the Anti-Recidivist Effort (ARE).

The focus of the program was still on cocaine mothers, but it had become part of an organized, established effort to address other substance abuse problems and patients. At the same time, greater control was exerted. A full-time staff position replaced the "peer counselor" position. A disciplinary regime was clearly posted and enforced. There was increased supervision and structure. The budget came from federal grants as well as local sources and donations. The process of revising and redoing the program sustained it. But after more than 5 years, Hope House no longer provides shelter for crack mothers and their babies. It was closed in 1996 because of lack of funding.

Epilogue

Crackworld survives in the midst of ruin. The subculture thrives on the underside of United States society. Poverty, degradation, and loss of hope encourage the lifestyle. For the greater number of U.S. citizens, Crackworld is a dimly understood reality. Fear was the response to the problems associated with this subculture as most people understood it. Fear was fueled by media images of African Americans in various stages of the criminal justice system for crack-related crimes. Laws and policies were enacted in a panic about crack, and law enforcement efforts were directed mostly at street crimes in black communities. The impact of these laws has been racist: Mandatory minimum sentencing laws against dealer/users are applied mostly to black people; crack mothers facing criminal penalties are mostly black; and most children taken from the custody of their families are black. Fundamental conflicts have been created in the system of justice, and these conflicts are leading in the direction of future crisis and chaos.

How crack mothers are treated now will lay the foundation for treatment of substance abusing mothers of whatever kind in the future.

Unless the problem of addiction is redefined in socioeconomic terms, there is little hope for positive change. The costs of our neglect are astronomical, and health care for infants born addicted is only one small part. The costs for education, health care, housing, and social services continue to rise, whereas resources allotted to these basics continue to decline.

Without means or reasons for change, the residents of Crackworld are likely to live out their lives in despair. In the midst of hopelessness, one substance or another will continue to be popular if it provides oblivion. There always will be a market in the underside of society for a drug that allows the residents to forget. The only way to rid society of crackworlds in the future is to get rid of the ruin, decay, and degradation on which they thrive.

Long-range solutions to the problems of Crackworld are clear and not impossible to achieve, but they go beyond providing for the special needs of women who use crack. The solutions rest with the systems of employment, education, justice, health care, family, and community social services. These are the systems that are in chaos in the neighborhoods where crackworlds thrive. These systems provide the basics of life; it is important that they be restored and supported. Programs to rebuild community life not only benefit substance abusers but also have a much wider impact. They are treatment options aimed at longer-range solutions. The costs for restoring social services and delivering opportunities to residents of the underside of United States society are high, but the benefits to be derived from this treatment option are without measure.

References

Abadinsky, H. (1989). *Drug abuse: An introduction*. Chicago: Nelson-Hall.

Alterman, A. I., O'Brien, C. P., & Droba, M. (1993). Day hospital vs. inpatient rehabilitation of cocaine abusers: An interim report. In F. Tims & C. Leukefeld (Eds.), *Cocaine treatment: Research and clinical perspectives* (pp. 150-162). Rockville, MD: National Institute on Drug Abuse.

Appel, D. (1992). Drug use during pregnancy: State strategies to reduce the prevalence of prenatal drug exposure. *The University of Florida Journal of Law and Public Policy, 1*, 105-145.

Bagley, K., & Merlo, A. (1995). Controlling women's bodies. In A. Merlo & J. Pollock (Eds.), *Women, law, and social control* (pp. 154-165). Boston: Allyn & Bacon.

Besharov, D. J. (1990a, July/August). Crack and kids: Children and their caretakers revisited. *Society*, pp. 25-26.

Besharov, D. J. (1990b, July/August). Crack children in foster care. *Children Today*, pp. 21-25.

Blumstein, A. (1995). *Youth violence, guns and illicit drug markets* [Videotape]. (Available from National Institute of Justice, Washington, DC)

Bourgois, P., & Dunlap, E. (1993). Exorcising sex-for-crack: An ethnographic perspective from Harlem. In M. S. Ratner (Ed.), *Crack pipe as pimp* (pp. 97-132). New York: Macmillan.

79

Boyle, K., & Anglin, D. M. (1993). "To the curb": Sex bartering and drug use among homeless crack users in Los Angeles. In M. S. Ratner (Ed.), *Crack pipe as pimp* (pp. 159-186). New York: Macmillan.

Brazil, J., & Salamone, D. (1991, April 19). Cocaine-mom ruling sets state precedent. *Orlando Sentinel*, p. A1.

Bureau of Justice Statistics. (1992). *Drugs, crime, and the justice system* (NCJ-133652). Washington, DC: Bureau of Justice Statistics, U.S. Department of Justice.

Carroll, K. M. (1992). Psychotherepy for cocaine abuse: Approaches, evidence and conceptual models. In T. Kosten & H. Kleber (Eds.), *Clinician's guide to cocaine addiction* (pp. 290-313). New York: Guilford.

Center for Substance Abuse Treatment. (1994). *Practical approaches in the treatment of women who abuse alcohol and other drugs*. Rockville, MD: Government Printing Office.

Chasnoff, I. (1989a). Cocaine, pregnancy, and the neonate. *Women and Health, 15*, 23-35.

Chasnoff, I. (1989b). Temporal patterns of cocaine use in pregnancy: Perinatal outcomes. *Journal of the American Medical Association, 261*, 1741-1744.

Cocaine babies are hurt more by environment. (1991, November/December). *Counselor*, p. 4.

Cocaine-exposed babies responsible for more than $500 million a year in hospital costs. (1991, October 21). *Monday Morning Review*, p. 1.

Coletti, S., Kim, S., Newel, R., & MacDonald, L. (1995). *A long-term outcome evaluation of a drug treatment program for women with children: The PAR Village experiment*. Unpublished report, Operation PAR, St. Petersburg, FL.

Commonwealth v. Welch, #92-SC-490-DG, 864 S.W.2d. 280 (1993). Kentucky.

Cox v. Court of Common Pleas, No. 88AP-856, 537 N.E.2d 722 (1988). Ohio.

Curriden, M. (1990). Holding mom accountable. *American Bar Journal, 76*(March), 50-53.

Daytona Beach News Journal, July 14, 1989, p. 3A.

DeLeon, G. (1993). Cocaine abusers in therapeutic community treatment. In F. Tims & C. Leukefeld (Eds.), *Cocaine treatment: Research and clinical perspectives* (pp. 163-189). Rockville, MD: National Institute on Drug Abuse.

Fallon, S. (1990, June). Drug abuse claims baby addicts. *State Government News, 33*(6), 8-10.

Feldman, H., Espada, F., Penn, S., & Byrd, S. (1993). Street status and the sex-for-crack scene in San Francisco. In M. S. Ratner (Ed.), *Crack pipe as pimp* (pp. 133-158). New York: Macmillan.

Frank, D., Zuckerman, B., Amaro, H., Aboagye, K., Bauchner, H., & Cabral, H. (1988). Cocaine use during pregnancy: Prevalence and correlates. *Pediatrics, 82*, 888-895.

Freeman, R. Rodriguez, G., & French, J. (1994). A comparison of male and female intravenous drug users' risk behaviors for HIV infection. *AM.J. Drug and Alcohol Abuse, 20* (2), 129-157.

French, J. F. (1993). Pipe dreams: Crack and the life in Philadelphia and Newark. In M. S. Ratner (Ed.), *Crack pipe as pimp* (pp. 205-232). New York: Macmillan.

Garcia, S., & Keilitz, I. (1990, July/August). Involuntary civil commitment of drug dependent persons with special reference to pregnant women. *Medical and Physical Law Representative*, pp. 418-426.

Gest, T. (1989, February). The pregnancy police on patrol. *U.S. News and World Report*, p. 50.

Goldstein, P. J., Belluci, P. A., Spunt, B. J., & Miller, T. (1991). Volume of cocaine use and violence. *Journal of Drug Issues, 21*, 345-367.

Grabowski, J., Higgins, S. T., & Kirby, K. C. (1993). Behavioral treatments of cocaine dependence. In F. Tims & C. Leukefeld (Eds.), *Cocaine treatment: Research and clinical perspectives* (pp. 133-149). Rockville, MD: National Institute on Drug Abuse.

Hatcher, C. (1992, July 24). State court overturns mother's conviction in cocaine baby case. *West Palm Beach Post*, pp. 1A.

Havassy, B. E., Wasserman, D. A., & Hall, S. M. (1993). Relapse to cocaine use: Conceptual issues. In F. Tims & C. Leukefeld (Eds.), *Cocaine treatment: Research and clinical perspectives* (pp. 203-217). Rockville, MD: National Institute on Drug Abuse.

Horowitz, R. (1990, July/August). Perinatal substance abuse. *Children Today*, pp. 9-12.

Howard, V. (1989, September 24). Drugs ravage neighborhood. *Daytona Beach News Journal*, p. A1.

Humphries, D. (1993). Mothers and children, drugs and crack: Reactions to maternal drug dependency. In R. Muraskin & T. Alleman (Eds.), *It's a crime: Women and justice* (pp. 130-145). Englewood Cliffs, NJ: Regents/Prentice Hall.

Inciardi, J. A. (1992). *The war on drugs II*. Mountain View, CA: Mayfield.

Inciardi, J. A. (1993). Sex, drugs and public policy. In M. S. Ratner (Ed.), *Crack pipe as pimp* (pp. 37-68). New York: Macmillan.

Inciardi, J. A., Lockwood, D., & Pottieger, A. E. (1993). Women, crack, and crime. In *Women and crack cocaine*. (107-135). New York: Macmillan.

Inciardi, J. A., Pottieger, A., & Surrat, H. (1996). African Americans and the crack-crime connection. In D. Chitwood, J. Rivers, & J. Inciardi (Eds.), *The American pipe dream* (pp. 56-70). Fort Worth, TX: Harcourt Brace College Publishers.

Jessup, M., & Roth, R. (1988). Clinical and legal perspectives on prenatal drug and alcohol use: Guidelines for individual and community response. *Medicine and Law, 7*, 3-12.

Johnson, B. D., Williams, T., Dei, K. A., & Sanabria, H. (1990). Drug abuse in the inner city: Impact on hard-drug users and the community. In M. Tonry & J. Wilson (Eds.), *Drugs and crime* (p. 14). Chicago: University of Chicago Press.

Johnson, D. N., & Vocci, F. J. (1993). Medications development at the National Institute on Drug Abuse: Focus on cocaine. In F. Tims & C. Leukefeld (Eds.), *Cocaine treatment: Research and clinical perspectives* (pp. 57-70). Rockville, MD: National Institute on Drug Abuse.

Johnson, P. (1990). The ACLU philosophy and the right to abuse the unborn. *Criminal Justice Ethics, 9*, 48-51.

Johnson v. State, 578 So.2d 419 (Fla. Alp. 5 Dist.) (1991).

Jolin, A. (1994). On the backs of working prostitutes: Feminist theory and prostitution policy. *Crime and Delinquency, 4*(1), 119-132.

Kantrowitz, B. (1989, October 2). Cocaine babies: The littlest victims. *Newsweek*, pp. 62-63.

Kasinsky, R. (1993). Criminalizing of pregnant women drug abusers. In C Culliver (Ed.), *Female criminality* (pp. 483-501). New York: Garland.

Khalsa, E. M., Paredes, A., & Anglin, D. M. (1993). Combinations of treatment modalities and therapeutic outcome for cocaine dependence. In F. Tims & C. Leukefeld (Eds.), *Cocaine treatment: Research and clinical perspectives* (pp. 237-259). Rockville, MD: National Institute on Drug Abuse.

Kleber, H. D. (1994). *Assessment and treatment of cocaine-abusing methadone-maintained patients*. Rockville, MD: Department of Health and Human Services.

Koester, S., & Schwartz, J. (1993). Crack, gangs, sex, and powerlessness: A view from Denver. In M. S. Ratner (Ed.), *Crack pipe as pimp* (pp. 187-204). New York: Macmillan.

Kosten, T. R. (1991). Client issues in drug abuse treatment: Addressing multiple drug abuse. In R. Pickens, C. Leukefeld, & C. Schuster (Eds.), *Improving drug abuse treatment* (NIDA Research Monograph 106). Rockville, MD: National Institute on Drug Abuse.

Levy, S., & Rutter, E. (1992). *Children of drug abusers*. New York: Lexington.

Lewin, T. (1987, November 23). Courts acting to force care on the unborn. *The New York Times*, p. A1.

Logli, P. (1990). Drugs in the womb: The newest battlefield in the war on drugs. *Criminal Justice Ethics, 9*, 23-29.

Lyman, M., & Potter, G. (1991). *Drugs in society: Causes, concepts and control*. Cincinnati: Anderson.

Maguire, K., & Pastore, A. (1994). *Sourcebook of criminal justice statistics*. Washington, DC: U.S. Department of Justice.

Maher, L., & Curtis, R. (1995). In search of the female urban "gangsta": Change, culture, and crack cocaine. In R. Price & N. Sokoloff (Eds.), *The criminal justice system and women* (2nd ed., pp. 147-166). New York: McGraw-Hill.

Mariner, W., Glantz, L., & Annas, G. (1990). Pregnancy, drugs and the perils of prosecution. *Criminal Justice Ethics, 9*, 30-40.

Marquez, P., Tippetts, A., & Branch, D. (1993). Cocaine in the hair of mother-infant pairs. *American Journal of Alcohol Abuse, 19*, 159-175.

McBride, D., & Rivers, J. (1996). Crack and crime. In D. Chitwood, J. Rivers, & J. Inciardi (Eds.), *The American pipe dream* (pp. 33-55). Ft. Worth, TX: Harcourt Brace College Publishers.

Merlo, A. (1993). Pregnant substance abusers: The new female offender. In R. Muraskin & T. Alleman (Eds.), *It's a crime: Women and justice* (pp. 146-160). Englewood Cliffs, NJ: Regents/Prentice Hall.

Metsch, L., McCoy, H., & Weatherby, N. (1996). Women and crack. In D. Chitwood, J. Rivers, & J. Inciardi (Eds.), *The American pipe dream* (pp. 71-88). Ft. Worth, TX: Harcourt Brace College Publishers.

Miller, G. (1989). *Born hooked: Confronting the impact of perinatal substance abuse*. Washington, DC: U.S. House of Representatives, Select Committee on Children, Youth, and Families.

Mills, C., & Bishop, L. (1990). Should pregnant women be held criminally liable for substance abuse? *State Government News, 3*(6), 22-23.

Morley, J. (1995, December 4-10). Crack in black and white. *Washington Post National Weekly Edition*, pp. 21-22.

Moses, M. (1995). Keeping incarcerated mothers and daughters together: Girl scouts beyond bars. (*NIJ Program Focus*, National Institute of Justice Publication #156217). Rockville, MD: National Institute of Justice, U.S. Department of Justice.

Musto, D. (1991). The history of legislative control over opium, cocaine and their derivatives. In R. Hamowy (Ed.), *Dealing with drugs* (pp. 37-71). San Francisco: Pacific Research Institute.

Myers, B., Olson, H., & Kaltenback, K. (1992, August/September). Cocaine-exposed infants: Myths and misunderstandings. *Zero to Three, 92*(1), 1-5.

National Institute of Justice. (1990). *Drug use forecasting annual report*. Washington, DC: Government Printing Office.

National Institute on Drug Abuse. (1991). *Summary of findings from 1991 National Household Survey on Drug Abuse* (NIDA Capsules C-86-13). Rockville, MD: Press Office of NIDA, U.S. Department of Health and Human Services.

Nelson, L. J., & Milliken, N. (1988). Compelled medical treatment of pregnant women: Life, liberty, and law in conflict. *Journal of the American Medical Association, 259*(7), 1060-1066.

New York Senate Committee on Investigations, Taxation and Government Operations. (1989). *Crack babies: The shame of New York*. Albany: New York Senate.

O'Brien, C. P., Ehrman, R. N., & Ternes, J. W. (1993). Developing treatments that address classical conditioning. In F. Tims & C. Leukefeld (Eds.), *Cocaine treatment: Research and clinical perspectives* (pp. 71-91). Rockville, MD: National Institute on Drug Abuse.

Office of National Drug Control Policy. (1995). *National drug control strategy*. Washington, DC: Executive Office of the President.

O'Keefe, N. (1989). *Special cocaine report*. St. Paul, MN: Chemical Abuse/Addiction Treatment Outcome Registry.

Osborn, J. E., Chair. (1990). *Report number four: HIV disease in correctional facilities*. Washington, DC: National Commission on Aids.

O'Sullivan, M. J., & Dooley, S. (1990). Many disagree with punitive approach to stemming drug abuse during pregnancy. *ACOG Newletter, 34*(May), 1.

Ouellet, L. J., Wiebel, W. W., Jimenez, A., & Johnson, W. (1993). Crack cocaine and the transformation of prostitution in three Chicago neighborhoods. In M. S. Ratner (Ed.), *Crack pipe as pimp* (pp. 69-96). New York: Macmillan.

Paltrow, L. M. (1990). When becoming pregnant is a crime. *Criminal Justice Ethics, 9*, 41-47.

The People of the State of New York v. Melissa A. Morabito, 580 NY S. 2d 843 (1992).

People v. Hardy, Michigan #128458, 469 N.W.2d. 50 (1991).

A prior priority: Early childhood. (1991, December 8). *The New York Times*, p. A16.

Quinney, R. (1970). *The social reality of crime*. Boston: Little, Brown.

Rangel, C. (1986). *The crack cocaine crisis* (Joint Hearing of Select Committee on Narcotics Abuse and Control and Select Committee on Children, Youth, and Families). Washington, DC: U.S. House of Representatives.

Ratner, M. S. (1993). Sex, drugs, and public policy: Studying and understanding the sex-for-crack phenomenon. In M. S. Ratner (Ed.), *Crack pipe as pimp* (pp. 1-36). New York: Macmillan.

Rawson, R. A., Obert, J. L., McCann, M. J., Smith, D. P., & Ling, W. (1993). Neurobehavioral treatment for cocaine dependency. In F. Tims & C. Leukefeld (Eds.), *Cocaine treatment: Research and clinical perspectives* (pp. 92-115). Rockville, MD: National Institute on Drug Abuse.

Reed, S. (1993). The criminalization of pregnancy: Drugs, alcohol and AIDs. In R. Muraskin & T. Alleman (Eds.), *It's a crime: women and justice* (pp. 93-117). Englewood Cliffs, NJ: Regents/Prentice Hall.

Robin-Vergeer, B. (1990). The problem of the drug-exposed newborn: A return to principled intervention. *The Stanford Law Review, 42*, 745-809.

Sagatun, I. (1993). Babies born with drug addiction. In R. Muraskin & T. Alleman (Eds.), *It's a crime: Women and justice* (pp. 118-129). Englewood Cliffs, NJ: Regents/Prentice Hall.

Schottenfeld, R. S., Carroll, K., & Rounsaville, B. (1993). Comorbid psychiatric disorders and cocaine abuse. In F. Tims & C. Leukefeld (Eds.), *Cocaine treatment: Research and clinical perspectives* (pp. 31-47). Rockville, MD: National Institute on Drug Abuse.

Scott, G. (1991, November). High cost of crack babies. *News Monitor*, p. 1

Spatz-Widom, C. (1989, April). The cycle of violence. *Science, 244,* 160-165.

Spitzer, B. (1987). A response to cocaine babies: Amendment of Florida's child abuse and neglect laws to encompass infants born drug dependent. *Florida State University Law Review, 15,* 865-884.

State v. Gethers, 585 So. 2d 1140, Fla. App. 4th Dist. (1991).

Tims, F., & Leukefeld, C., (Eds.). (1993). *Cocaine treatment: Research and clinical perspectives.* Rockville, MD: National Institute on Drug Abuse.

U.S. House of Representatives Select Committee on Children, Youth, and Families. (1990). *Fact sheet: Women, addiction and perinatal substance abuse.* Washington, DC: U.S. House of Representatives.

U.S. v. Dumas, 64 F.3d 1427 (9th Cir., 1995).

Washton, A. M. (1988). Preventing relapse to cocaine. *The Journal of Clinical Psychiatry, 49*(2, Suppl.), 34-38.

Webster v. Reproductive Health Services, 492 U.S. 490, 519 (1989).

Weiss, R. D., Mirin, S. M., Griffin, M. L., & Michael, J. (1988). Psychopathology in chronic cocaine abusers. *Journal of Nervous and Mental Disorders, 176,* 719-725.

Wilkins, W., (Chair). (1993, November 9). *Hearing on crack cocaine* (U.S. Sentencing Commission). Washington, DC: Miller Reporting.

Williams, T. (1992). *Crackhouse.* New York: Penguin.

Woolredge, J. D., & Masters, K. (1993). Confronting problems faced by pregnant inmates in state prisons. *Crime and Delinquency, 39,* 195-203.

Zinberg, N. E. (1984). *Drug, set, and setting: The basis for controlled intoxicant use.* New Haven, CT: Yale University Press.

Zuckerman, B., Frank, D., Hingson, R., Amaro, H., Levenson, S., & Kayne, H. (1989). Effects of maternal marijuana and cocaine use on fetal growth. *The New England Journal of Medicine, 320*(12), 762-768.

Index

About the Author

Sue Mahan is the coordinator for the criminal justice program at the University of Central Florida at Daytona Beach. After completing her dissertation, *Case Study of a Woman's Prison*, at the New Mexico State Corrections Center for Women, she received her Ph.D. from the University of Missouri, Columbia. Mahan is the author of a book published by R&E titled *Unfit Mothers* and the coauthor of a book with Ralph Weisheit for Anderson titled *Women, Crime and Criminal Justice*. Her research interests include family violence and cross-cultural studies. During 1996, she served as a Fulbright scholar at Universidad de Lima in Peru.